PHILANTHROPY
AND CULTURE

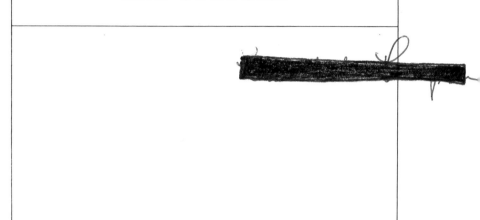

PHILANTHROPY AND CULTURE

The International Foundation Perspective

E D I T E D   B Y

Kathleen D. McCarthy

Published for The Rockefeller Foundation by the University of Pennsylvania Press · Philadelphia

Library of Congress Cataloging in Publication Data

Main entry under title:

Philanthropy and culture.

 Papers presented at a conference sponsored by the
Rockefeller Foundation held in Bellagio, Italy, 1981.
 Bibliography: p.
 1. Humanities—Endowments—Congresses. I. McCarthy,
Kathleen D. II. Rockefeller Foundation.
AS911.A2P49 1984   060   84-2356
ISBN 0-8122-1173-1 (pbk.)

Printed in the United States of America
Designed by Adrianne Onderdonk Dudden

Contents

Preface   *vii*

Acknowledgments   *xv*

PART ONE: VIEW FROM THE UNITED STATES

Introduction

KATHLEEN D. McCARTHY
1   *U.S. Foundations and International Concerns*   3

MALCOLM RICHARDSON
2   *The Humanities and International Understanding: Some
Reflections on the Experience of the Rockefeller Foundation*   25

W. McNEIL LOWRY
3   *Humanism and the Humanities: An Effort at Definition*   42

DANELLA SCHIFFER
4   *Business Support of the Humanities: A Global Perspective*   55

5   *Discussions*   65

PART TWO: THE INTERNATIONAL SCENE

Introduction

KATHLEEN D. McCARTHY
6   *Non-U.S. Foundations: An Overview*   85

RONALD C. TRESS
7   *British Foundations and the Humanities*   102

OTTO HÄFNER
8   *Foundations and Government Support for the Humanities in
Germany*   113

KAZUE IWAMOTO

9 *An Overview of Japanese Philanthropy and International Cooperation in the Third World* 122

FRANCIS X. SUTTON

10 *Foundations and Cultural Development of the Third World* 137

11 *Discussions* 156

Conclusions 176

Biographical Sketches of Contributors 181

List of Participants 183

Bibliographical Essay 184

Preface

Twentieth-century observers often note the increasingly stark division between C. P. Snow's "two cultures." Humanistic concerns tend to be dismissed as the intellectual baggage of a gentler, less complicated era: interesting pursuits for isolated coteries of intellectuals, but clearly separate from the mainstream of contemporary life. Science and technical expertise, rather than the humanities, are revered as present and future oracles. This dichotomy permeates the thinking of industrialized nations and has begun to typify the efforts of policy makers in less-developed areas as well. In government, education, and business the primary emphasis is on managerial know-how and technological skills.

Philanthropy, too, has evinced a marked drift toward vocational, practical, scientific, and technically grounded concerns. Only a handful of U.S. foundations support humanistic endeavors, a pattern echoed among the growing ranks of Asian, Latin American, and European foundations. In order to survey the extent of international foundation development and to assay the prospects for privately funded humanistic ventures in the United States and abroad, the Rockefeller Foundation convened a five-day conference on International Philanthropy and the Humanities at the Villa Serbelloni, the foundation's conference center in Bellagio, Italy, in autumn 1981.

The conference was unique in that it brought together foundation spokespersons from five continents to consider one of the most neglected and least visible areas of international largesse: the humanities. The participants represented a variety of backgrounds and interests and ranged from professionally trained humanists to social activists involved in the development process. All were or had at one time been employed by foundations. The sessions were as diverse as the roster of participants, centering on American, European, and Third World cultural endeavors, foundation development, the shifting balance of responsibility between public and private funders, and the appropriate role of foundations and humanists in the development process.

The justification for devoting resources to cultural concerns was a recurrent question. Why focus on cultural resources, particularly in an era still vexed by problems of basic human survival and overshadowed by the threat of nuclear holocaust? Several justifications were posited. As one participant noted, humanistic study undergirds and often anticipates many contemporary social and scientific concerns. It can illuminate value systems and trace the roots of social issues and societal ills. In less-developed areas, cultural research can help to define the national character of new nations, foster a sense of collective identity, and in the case of linguistics, often forms an important framework for national educational policy making. Historical and religious studies, literature, philosophy, linguistics, cultural preservation, and anthropology—all have contributed in some way to the development process. Perhaps the most eloquent defense was that of Francis X. Sutton of the Ford Foundation, who maintained that

> there is a false dichotomy in suggesting that we must make a radical choice between attending to the basic economic needs of a people and their humanistic needs, unless we are reduced to relief measures and simply fighting famine and disaster. Most Third World peoples are not going to get rich in our time. They are not going to be relieved of serious problems, and we are not going to lift everybody to the GNP per capita of Sweden or Germany. Yet their lives must be made worthwhile in their own time.

Despite their potential importance, the humanities and cultural preservation have been overlooked by the majority of foundation programs both in the United States and abroad. Although foundations have been established at a quickening pace throughout the world, most have turned their attention to policy issues and scientific research. Similarly, only a few U.S. foundations are active in the humanities, and even these devote only a fraction of their total budgets to humanistic concerns. As foundation spokesmen noted in the unpublished 1949 Gaither report ("Report of the Study for the Ford Foundation on Policy and Program," Ford Foundation MSS, Ford Foundation, New York), which lay at the heart of Ford's reorganization and rise to international prominence after 1950, "a history of philanthropic support for the humanities may bear the subtitle, 'The Short and Simple Annals of the Poor'" (p. 23).

Each of the conference papers addresses these issues from a different perspective. W. McNeil Lowry, who headed the Ford Foundation's highly successful Humanities and Arts program, explores the meaning, role, and relevance of international humanistic philanthropy, with particular emphasis on the politically sensitive issues inherent in such work. Citing the example of a Ford program to keep cultural inquiry alive within a European totalitarian state, he observes that "the essence of the humanities is the ability to make choices," a matter which some governments and quasi-political groups would prefer to obscure. Nor is this problem confined to foreign areas. Noting the secular humanism outburst in the United States, Lowry concludes that free thought, democracy, and individual liberty can be fostered by ensuring the survival and well-being of those most complex, value-laden realms of human inquiry, the humanities.

Malcolm Richardson's essay outlines some of the specific ways in which the humanities might be fostered. Focusing on the Rockefeller Foundation's humanistic endeavors, he details the history of the foundation's involvement in the support of creative writing and translation programs, individual research, scholarly exchanges, library development—as he explains, "the ways of helping are almost endless." Richardson also discusses the foundation's ongoing commitment to the notion that cultural exchange can foster intercultural understanding as a necessary prelude to the maintenance of a healthy world order. As he points out, "For any real understanding between nations, and not only in the sense of diplomatic entente but in the deeper sense of mutual comprehension and respect, the study of language, literature, philosophy, and history is essential." These studies not only encourage, but make possible, intercultural dialogue, cooperation, and exchange.

Francis X. Sutton adopts a still broader view. Moving beyond the traditional scholarly disciplines which were the target of the Rockefeller Foundation's work, Sutton details the Ford Foundation's experiences with nonacademically oriented programs in developing countries, particularly cultural preservation, and presents the need for greater foundation involvement in this "little-worked and uncrowded field." As he explains, "Parts of a culture and indeed whole traditions are constantly being left behind and lost." Warning of the need to prevent a "retreat into a surly parochialism," Sutton points out that "there must be scholars, technicians, artists, intellectuals, educators, and indeed cultural propagandists who devote themselves to sorting and saving." As he noted in a paper called "Cultural Implications of Aid Programs," delivered at the Truman International Conference on Technical

Assistance and Development at Hebrew University, Jerusalem, in May 1970, if nations

> do not develop their own art, music and literature, they will lose what they have in a flood of magazines, paperbacks, records, and transistor radios. If they do not write their own history and philosophy, they will read it in the works of curious and industrious outsiders who will become, embarrassingly, authorities and interpreters for them. The preservation and the autonomous development of a national culture . . . must proceed within general ideas and techniques that are part of the world's cosmopolitan culture. [P. 15]

The ambitious efforts of the Ford and Rockefeller foundations contrast vividly with the guarded corporate prognosis posited by Danella Schiffer. As Schiffer points out, corporate support of humanistic undertakings at home or abroad has been relatively insignificant, since "this area is seen as having little relevance to a corporation's well-being." If humanists have hopes of garnering corporate support for their endeavors, they will have to state their case more clearly, more eloquently, and with greater force, underscoring the relevance of their work to the business world. As Schiffer explains, companies "tend to favor those issues and causes which are related to their business." Thus, "humanists must be willing to market the humanities" if they wish to benefit from the ongoing expansion of corporate philanthropy. This paper generated some lively disagreements at the conference, as might be expected. Many of the participants, particularly those with advanced degrees in the humanities, found Schiffer's ideas somewhat startling, if not distasteful. However, it would be wrong to underestimate the importance of the corporate view. At a time when the U.S. government is attempting to cut back on public funding across the board, and particularly in the area of cultural support, her views are especially relevant. If government funding and the assets of the nation's private foundations diminish, corporate philanthropy will become an increasingly important component of the total funding scene. This reapportionment of responsibility has implications for every type of nonprofit activity, including the humanities.

The essays which deal with non-U.S. activities present an interesting admixture of optimism, ingenuity, and dismay. Like Schiffer's, each underscores the point that prospects for the humanities are severely limited. As Ronald Tress explains, "At best, they are a minority interest [among British funders]; for most, they are of no interest at all." The international scene is bleaker still, for "British institutions with a commitment to the arts and humanities are few, and those with horizons beyond Britain's shores are fewer." Moreover, governmental allocations for humanistic work have remained small and will probably remain so in the future, a difficulty that raises the need to combine "academic innovation in subjects and in methods with conditions of zero growth."

Otto Häfner's essay echoes many of Tress's concerns, and outlines some of the ways in which Germany's largest foundation has attempted to cope with governmental retrenchment. In contrast to the situation in Britain, where, as Tress points out, the humanities have been a minority interest among funders, some of the largest German foundations, including Volkswagen and Thyssen, devote significant amounts of their resources to humanistic concerns. The Tress and Häfner essays raise several important issues of central concern to American and international foundations: the appropriate role of foundations vis-à-vis government funding, the need or desirability of taking up projects which the government has abandoned, the problems posed by these trends for foundations' traditional work as innovators and pioneers.

Kazue Iwamoto's essay presents a general overview of the Japanese situation. Most Japanese foundations, including Toyota, are of recent origin, founded since the beginning of the 1970s. Foundation philanthropy is a transplanted idea which the Japanese are grafting onto the country's cultural, social, and academic scene. Most Japanese foundations are small by U.S. standards, and the humanities have played a limited role in their programs, because, as Iwamoto explains, the government does not currently allow deductions for charitable gifts to international or cultural concerns. Nevertheless, a few foundations, like Toyota, have developed innovative programs in the humanities, and others may follow if the laws are changed. The most important point of this essay addresses the issue of scale. Toyota's "Know Our Neighbors" Translation-Publication Program, developed over the course of the last six years under Iwamoto's direction, clearly demonstrates that there is a role for small, carefully managed and constructed foundation programs which parallel the more massive undertakings of giants like the Ford Foundation, UNESCO, and national governments. As Iwamoto explains, "Different kinds of programs [are] suitable for different sizes of organizations. If we overlooked this point, we would tend to make only quantitative comparisons and would fail to grasp the real situation." The Toyota Foundation's example provides a useful counterpoint to the large-scale undertakings outlined in the essays on the Volkswagen, Rockefeller, and Ford foundations and illustrates fresh models for the many small foundations which are now developing throughout the world.

The conference discussions elaborated upon these issues and concerns. Lowry's presentation quickly divided the group into pessimists who framed the issues in disciplinary and academic terms and optimists who rejected the "garrison mentality" of their concerned peers. Pointing to declining enrollments in the humanities, receding career opportunities, and shrinking funds, the pessimists sketched a bleak picture of the humanities in the United States, Europe, and Australia. Led by Francis X. Sutton, Raymond Georis, and Tadashi Yamamoto, the optimist camp painted a more cheerful scenario, citing the growing public demand for humanistic learning outside the academy. Soaring museum attendance, thriving commercial outlets, and the growing potential for media exploitation of traditional humanistic themes all indicate a healthy public interest in history, literature, and related fields. Participants from underdeveloped areas added a third voice, calling for a rapprochement between ivory-tower scholars and the larger populace through village-level programs carefully integrated with development aims.

Funding was a second theme. All the participants agreed that the humanities were among the least competitive contenders for shrinking governmental and private resources. Accordingly, several suggestions were made about ways in which humanists might strengthen their case—or even their programs—through innovative means. For example, corporations might be "seduced" by programs promising high visibility and significant returns, such as archaeological digs, exhibitions, and media programs. Loaned expertise and technology, including donated computer time, might help to improve the cost-effectiveness of some types of humanistic endeavor, as might efforts to strengthen traditional market mechanisms—the publishing industry and university presses. Belen Abreu, citing the experience of her own organization, the Ramon Magsaysay Award Foundation, as a prime example, raised the point that programs should be made self-supporting wherever possible.

Waldemar A. Nielsen's commentary carefully detailed the changing U.S. funding scene and outlined several possible roles for foundation activity as governmental funding sources contract. Noting that governments in industrialized nations currently supply upwards of 90 percent of the available funding for the humanities, he discussed the issues of politicization, the increasing dependency of recipient organizations, and the potentially devastating effect of public retrenchment. Questions of how to provide for the next generation of scholars, how to maintain employment opportunities for humanists outside the academy as university programs contract, how cultural endeavors might be made more competitive in the race for dwindling resources, and how foundations might protect themselves from falling into a conservationist role were also explored in this session.

In other sessions, foundations were warned of the pitfalls of cultural colonialism and urged to devise programs which would make scholarly findings available to policy makers and the populace at large. Citing the number of unemployed Ph.D.'s in Latin America, Enrique Fernandez attacked the university development programs of the 1960s for "selling hope," and suggested the preferability of more modest undertakings, a notion heartily seconded by Belen Abreu. As Abreu pointed out, people in poor countries are eager to preserve their own cultures, but must meet basic needs as well. Elitist culture embodied in university programs has little direct relevance for most of the populace. Part of the foundations' task should be to devise projects to make the fruits of humanistic scholarship and cultural preservation available to the general public. This task would entail small programs based on people-to-people contact, rather than massive reforms, and would teach people about their own culture, each other, and the world beyond in comprehensible terms.

Possibilities for foundation cooperation in achieving some of these goals were also discussed. Pointing to the advantages of joint ventures in depoliticizing Third World aid, Tadashi Yamamoto asked how mutually acceptable development priorities might be formulated and humanistic aims integrated into larger development strategies. In answer, inquiries into the activities of the World Bank and UNESCO were suggested. Georis, Fernandez, and Yamamoto concurred that foundations in Europe, Latin America, and Japan would be amenable to more cooperative ventures. The largest stumbling block for initiatives in the humanities, as in other fields, is the lack of information about what is currently being done, who is doing it, and what might be undertaken in the future. Needed information concerns not only the work of funding agencies and governments but humanists themselves. With more reliable information at hand about the scholarly resources available for such undertakings, foundations might be more willing to venture into this previously neglected terrain, both individually and in concert with donors from other lands.

The conference produced no ringing declaration, no neatly categorized shopping list of priorities for the 1980s, and, indeed, very little agreement about the health and future of the humanities. What it did achieve was an underscoring of the problems common to foundations throughout the world in an era of inflation, retrenchment, and increasing competition for dwindling funds. It reviewed past work in the humanities by foundations large and small, both in the United States and abroad, and tested the prospects for future efforts. In the process, it revealed with startling clarity that the humanities are indeed the poor relations of the nonprofit family, and are likely to remain so unless more effective means of publicizing their case can be devised. Prescriptions ranged from a more worldly approach to corporate funding to the provision of more sophisticated data on cultural endeavors for national and foreign donors, corporations, and development personnel. The conference provided a platform for vigorous Third World critiques of previous foundation efforts in the cultural arena and afforded new models for smaller enterprises scaled to fit the budgets of many of the world's new foundations. It revealed a bright strand of optimism concerning the adaptability of foundations and their ability to cooperate in areas of mutual concern. Finally, the Bellagio meeting underscored a deep and abiding faith in the ability of cultural study to contribute to mutual understanding and freedom of thought in today's increasingly complex and interdependent world.

Acknowledgments

Several people graciously assisted me in the course of developing this conference, bringing it to fruition, and assembling the proceedings. Joel Colton served as co-organizer, admirably chairing sessions and hosting the proceedings at Bellagio. Datus Smith, Jr., James Himes, Peter Ruof, Russell Phillips, William Moody, and Peter Kamura helped with their advice and suggestions; this conference, quite literally, could not have occurred without them. Subsequent conversations with Jose Blanco, Michel Pomey, Luisa M. de Pulido, Abdurrahman A. Bushnaq, Sheila Arvin McLean, Katherine McKee, Landrum Bolling, Robert Payton, William Orme, Roger Stone, and Kenneth Maxwell also helped to sharpen my perceptions of the international philanthropic scene. At Bellagio, Robert Celli and the staff did a magnificent job, ensuring that the conference ran smoothly, on time, and with great élan. My co-workers at the Rockefeller Foundation helped in ways too varied to enumerate. I particularly wish to thank Steven M. Cahn, Susan Garfield, Lynn A. Szwaja, Terry Little, Helen Bungert, Cathy Boston, and Priscilla Rieppl for their unflagging generosity and aid.

I owe a profound debt to the participants themselves, who turned my work into an exciting adventure. Danella Schiffer, Belen Abreu, Henry Cavanna, Enrique Fernandez, Raymond Georis, Giovanni Granaglia, Otto Häfner, Wolfgang Heisenberg, Kazue Iwamoto, Ian Lancaster, W. McNeil Lowry, Waldemar A. Nielsen, Gideon Paz, Nils-Eric Svensson, Ronald Tress, Erhardt Waespi, Meriel Wilmot, and Tadashi Yamamoto all deserve special thanks for their efforts, their ideas, and their camaraderie. My husband, Chris Olander, Malcolm L. Richardson, Frank Sutton, and Katherine Little deserve special mention, for they have helped this project through every stage since its inception, cheerfully offering advice, encouragement, assistance, and an occasional goad when most needed.

PART ONE

View from the United States

INTRODUCTION

International largesse has been one of the earmarks of U.S. foundation activities since the early decades of the twentieth century. Although best known for their achievements in the scientific arena, particularly agriculture, public health, and scientific research, foundations have also played an important (albeit limited) role in the promotion of the humanities. The essays and discussions in this section assess the rise of international foundation philanthropy and its implications for the humanities and broader cultural concerns from an unabashedly American perspective, examining general trends as well as the specific contributions of the Rockefeller and Ford foundations and the corporate community. The first essay, a general overview, is followed by three specific case studies: two of private foundations, one of corporate philanthropy.

The discussions following this group of essays add a governmental dimension to the issues, exploring the various stances foundations might adopt if public funding diminishes, comparing U.S. corporate developments with foreign trends, and examining the tension between university-based and outreach activities in the cultural arena. Both the discussions and the essays maintain a triple focus, on past and present foundation developments and their implications for the humanities, while tentatively beginning to test for points of convergence with non-U.S. grant makers. In the process, U.S. precedents, foreign counterpoints, and larger questions of worldwide responsibilities are explored.

1 / U.S. Foundations and International Concerns

KATHLEEN D. McCARTHY

American foundation achievements in the promotion of worldwide health and agricultural reform are well known. Less familiar, however, are their contributions to internationally oriented cultural endeavors, the manner in which humanities disciplines have meshed with larger development aims and national programmatic goals, and the ways in which patterns of support have evolved in recent years. The following essay examines these issues, with an eye to differences between private and corporate foundation funding, present needs, and possible areas of future support.

The notion that private philanthropy is an individual right and a personal imperative is deeply etched on the American psyche. From a modest beginning of sporadic individual voluntarism during the colonial era, U.S. philanthropic endeavors have grown to include a fully articulated system of local, national, and international nonprofit agencies. U.S. insistence on the inviolability of individual social action has helped to develop, nurture, and refine a variety of imported philanthropic forms, not the least of which is the modern foundation. Although charitable trusts had long existed in Europe and the Middle East, turn-of-the-century U.S. philanthropists restructured them in focus and form, nationalizing and internationalizing their work and shifting their goals from almsgiving to fundamental social change.

Several disparate influences contributed to the development of the modern foundation at the turn of the century. In addition to the cherished belief that Americans owed a debt of time and money to their communities, religious injunctions and the ongoing need to deal with the social ills generated in the wake of immigration, industrialization, and rapid urbanization gave added urgency to the philanthropists' tasks. Local imperatives meshed with national concerns, as the rise of corporations and the development of great fortunes lifted the philanthropists' range of vision from the local scene and gave them the means of dealing with problems on a national scale. At the same time, a new generation of reformers and social theorists who came to the fore in the 1890s began to sharpen the distinction between charity and philanthropy. Charity, the reformers announced, only temporarily ameliorated social ills. Research, expertise, flexibility, experimentation, and pioneering new programs which might then become the province of the state—these were the basic tenets of the new philanthropy. Rather than treating symptoms, philanthropy would find a cure.

The new philanthropic code had international, as well as national, implications. Americans had long cultivated the habit of giving abroad. Beginning in the early nineteenth century, citizens repeatedly organized spontaneous drives for disaster relief and generously funded the work of a welter of missionary societies. Foundations incorporated these traditions, secularizing the missionary impulse and wedding it to newer scientific ideals. Goaded by imaginative advisers such as Frederic T. Gates and Abraham Flexner, wealthy philanthropists like John D. Rockefeller shifted the focus of their giving from traditional, local, religious aims to international endeavors modeled upon the missionary experience and the bureaucratic structure of the modern business corporation.

Founded in 1913, Rockefeller's foundation quickly plunged into the heady task of international health reform. From its ambitious campaign to eradicate hookworm, to its program to make Peking Union Medical College into the "Johns Hopkins of China," to the "Green Revolution" of the post–World War II era, the foundation pursued its aims on a worldwide scale. In the process, the Rockefeller Foundation set the precedent for international foundation work via close collaboration with governments, a model which would continue to be pursued by a handful of the nation's largest foundations.

The Carnegie Corporation (founded in 1911) and the Ford Foundation also played an important role in spreading U.S. philanthropic ideals and largesse to a worldwide audience. Ford was by far the largest of the "big three." It began operations on a fairly modest scale in Michigan in 1936, the creation of the eccentric industrial genius Henry Ford and his son, Edsel. Initially it operated locally, funding the family's favorite charities. By 1948, however, company reorganizations, stipulations in Ford's will, and family considerations effected a basic realignment, precipitously lifting the foundation to national and international prominence and underwriting it on a hitherto-unimagined scale. A multivolume study commissioned by the trustees, headed by H. Rowan Gaither, and issued in 1950 heralded the arrival of this giant on the foundation scene. Citing the threat of nuclear war as the world's most pressing problem, Gaither advised the trustees to work on an international as well as a national scale, advice which was quickly implemented with an initial grant for Indian agricultural programs in 1951. Millions of dollars in grant monies would eventually pass through the hands of the foundation's staff as they expanded the scope of their operations first to Asia, Europe, and the Middle East and then to Africa, Latin America, and the Caribbean, eventually girdling the globe.

The birth of the Ford Foundation, like that of the Carnegie and the Rockefeller, must be viewed from the context of the times in order to be fully appreciated. In 1950 the world was just beginning to recuperate from the shocks and scars of the Second World War. This was the era of Joe McCarthy, civil defense, the Rosenbergs, and the spectacular Hiss trial. The nightmare of nuclear proliferation was rapidly becoming a reality as Communist and capitalist countries squared off and began laying out the ground rules for cold war. Colonialism had begun to falter and decay, leaving many territories with the hope of imminent independence and self-rule, while the war-torn countries of their former colonizers lay in ruins. Problems and possibilities for philanthropic endeavor abounded.

U.S. technology and ingenuity had unleashed the bomb. It was at this point hoped that the nation's technical genius could help, as well as destroy, in the brave new world of the mid-twentieth century. Hunger, disease, and ignorance no longer seemed tolerable, not only because worldwide communications developments brought these ills into view with renewed force but also because they now constituted an implied threat to international harmony and global security. Some areas seemed more in need of aid than others; India's case was particularly compelling. Plagued by repeated crop failures in the years immediately following World War II, India faced the grim prospect of widespread famine in which unprecedented numbers might have perished. Although rich in human resources, the newly independent nation lacked the capital and expertise to address its problems in a systematic way.

Accordingly, Ford Foundation personnel were tapped by Prime Minister Nehru to aid in the task of national agricultural reform.

Following an initial grant of $1.2 million to the government of India in 1951, foundation officials quickly swung into a fully elaborated program of community development, with particular emphasis on training agricultural extension workers to implement new farming techniques. In the best spirit of American philanthropy, India was to be taught to help itself. From a modest base in the nation's villages, the program quickly expanded to include efforts to strengthen the educational system, particularly agricultural colleges and facilities for training the managerial elites needed to run the country as colonial forces withdrew. Between 1951 and 1956, over $16 million was spent in India, 50 percent of which was siphoned into community-level projects.

Although the Indian programs remained the linchpin of Ford's international work until 1958, the foundation's interests had already begun to expand. By 1956 funds were being spent on agricultural, educational, and cultural programs in a variety of other new nations, including Pakistan, Burma, Indonesia, and areas of the Middle East. Over $41 million had been expended in these areas by the mid-1950s, that is, a 12–15 percent share of the foundation's total resources. As Ford's range of vision continued to broaden, sub-Saharan Africa was added to the list of recipients in 1958, and Latin America and the Caribbean in the 1960s. By the time the foundation celebrated its thirtieth anniversary, a staggering $1.7 billion had been funneled into international programs, $1 billion of which had been spent in the Third World.

The humanities played a peripheral role in these developments, amply funded when they dovetailed with the foundation's drive to enhance local managerial capabilities, ignored when they did not. One of the most generously funded areas was linguistic research, which meshed nicely with Ford's larger development aims. As former Ford staffer Melvin Fox explained, there was a "steadily increasing awareness on the part of external aid agencies—and the expatriate technical assistants supported by them—that 'modernization' cannot be achieved by a simple lateral transfer of knowledge, experience, and techniques."[1] Effective communication lay at the heart of the modernization process, whether one was dealing with basic education and the promotion of literacy or with instruction in the most sophisticated managerial and scientific techniques. Accordingly, the foundation launched a highly diversified program of language surveys, curricular development, research, and studies of the relationship of language to national goals. Although more than thirty-eight countries were ultimately included in this work, it had the greatest relevance for areas such as Tanzania, India, and the Philippines, where hotly debated linguistic issues played a central role in governmental attempts to forge a cohesive national identity and free their nations from the legacies of the colonial past.

Beginning with efforts to promote Teaching English as a Second Language (TESL), the main thrust of Ford's linguistic activities gradually evolved into a strong emphasis on a more effective usage of vernacular languages. The development of sociolinguistics in the 1960s, a growing recognition of the limitations of world languages in the development process, and a corollary rise in appreciation for the virtues of vernacular and bilingual instruction all contributed to this trend.

Other areas, such as cultural preservation, were less lavishly funded and more diffuse. Ford Foundation projects, most of which were concentrated in Asia and the Pacific, ranged from programs to train archaeologists, archivists, and museum personnel to maintain local treasures to a variety of oral history and archival programs. As Robert Mayer, assistant to the vice-president for administration, explained, it was a complex and challenging task, because the search for cultural identification

> takes one beyond the written history of a country. As we study the past in the developing world, we find that past emerging from music, dance, painting, sculpture, and not written documentation. The media for preservation of such heritages are not those that we are familiar with as archivists. We must record the music; we must film the dance patterns; we must clean and repair the paintings and sculptures. To do these things we turn to the museum curator, the documentary film producer, and the sound technician.[2]

The opposite side of the coin was Ford's determination to increase America's linguistic and analytical capabilities for other areas of the world, a vital corollary to the nation's rapid rise to world power following World War II. This step entailed preparing the nation to assume its role as a world leader and helping to promote intercultural understanding at home and abroad. To achieve this end, area studies centers were established at leading universities with Ford money, as well as substantial grants from its sister institutions, Rockefeller and Carnegie. Ford began its activities in the field with a study by the Board of Overseas Training and Research, a distinguished advisory group, which investigated American educational and research needs in international relations. Among its recommendations, the report counseled Ford to increase the number of American specialists, including historians and linguists, for a range of foreign areas; to fill the gaps for previously neglected geographical areas; and to help to disseminate this information to the public at large.

In the typical Ford fashion, this recommendation was followed by a series of stunningly large donations: $250,000 to the American Council of Learned Societies for a program in basic training and research for Near East studies; $2 million to the American University Field Service for scholarly exchanges; and a multi-university push to strengthen area studies centers for Asia, Africa, the Near East, and the Soviet Union. Between 1960 and 1967, when the program was phased down, the Ford Foundation provided over $200 million for research and the training of area studies specialists, and the humanities received an important share.

Each of the "big three" foundations approached the task of funding international humanities projects in its own way. African programs are a case in point. Africa provided ample opportunities for modernization programs of every stripe and hue. Of all the areas of the developing world, it is still the most needy. Sub-Saharan Africa is currently distinguished by high illiteracy rates; extreme ethnic diversity; political fragmentation; labor-intensive agricultural systems, many of which operate at the subsistence level; and a staggering rate of population growth. Africans have shorter lifespans, higher infant mortality rates, and lower incomes than their counterparts anywhere else in the world. Twenty of the world's thirty poorest countries are located south of the Sahara. These problems were compounded in the 1950s and 1960s as, one by one, former colonies were liberated from European rule. Ghana was granted independence in 1957, Nigeria in 1960, Tanzania in 1961, and Kenya in 1963. Few Africans had occupied positions of authority under the colonial system, and managers of all varieties had to be trained to fill freshly vacated posts in government, industry, and education. Health services had to be expanded and modernized, as did local agricultural techniques, which had persisted in the same mode for centuries.

Cultural research was an important component of the development process in the first years after independence. Postcolonial

Africans needed to reaffirm their national identities, both for themselves and for the rest of the world. This process entailed the formidable task of separating colonial legacies from things uniquely African. In the eyes of much of the world Africa was, to use Joseph Conrad's phrase, the "heart of darkness." Centuries of colonial domination had produced a powerful stereotype of a primitive world peopled by tribes with no past, no collective memory, no trace of a legitimate culture. Rather than tapping the riches of their own heritage, generations of young Africans had been taught to celebrate the foreign values embodied in European cultural forms.

Western scholars portrayed Africa as a historyless land, dating its past from the arrival of the first Europeans. The development of African historiography was hampered by the fact that much of the continent's past lies buried in tribal lore passed from one generation to the next. It is primarily an oral culture. In order to correct misguided notions about their culture, creative historians like Bethwell Ogot developed new means of gathering evidence, incorporating folk tales, artifacts, and tribal traditions via the combined skills of professional historians, anthropologists, archaeologists, and linguists. Since Ogot began his pioneering work almost three decades ago, increasing stores of Arabic, Hausa, and Swahili documents have been unearthed, adding to the world's knowledge of Africa's precolonial past.

Writers as well as historians worked to refine the world's vision of sub-Saharan Africa. Nigeria, in particular, produced an impressive store of talented authors, including Buchi Emecheta and Chinua Achebe, an early Rockefeller fellow. Unlike their earlier European counterparts, Achebe and Emecheta portray Nigeria as a country rich in tradition and marked by complex social structures. As Achebe explains, he has deliberately used his literary skills to "help my society regain its belief in itself and put away the complexes of years of denigration and self-denigration."[3]

Their work often underscores the power of indigenous impediments to the success of policy-oriented development work. Grace Ogot's *The Promised Land* carefully details the clash of modern medicine and deeply ingrained folk beliefs among the Luo of East Africa, while Buchi Emecheta's *The Joys of Motherhood* vividly delineates the values which hamper population-control efforts in Africa's most populous state. Emecheta's work reveals the extent of the changes which have to be made if the growth rate is to be curbed. Similarly, Achebe's *No Longer at Ease* and T. M. Aluko's *Kinsman and Foreman* are among the many literary works which graphically detail the clash of Western and indigenous values and educational norms.

All of these developments have direct relevance for foundation work. Carnegie, for example, has had a long-standing interest in African educational affairs. The Carnegie Corporation's efforts in Africa date from 1925, when a Jeanes School was set up in Kenya with a $37,500 grant from the corporation's Commonwealth Program. Based on U.S. educational techniques developed among rural blacks in the South and predicated upon the doctrines of Booker T. Washington and the curriculum at his Tuskegee Institute, Jeanes Schools placed a heavy emphasis on vocational, rather than classical, training. Deeply impressed with Washington's reports, the trustees of the Carnegie Corporation and the Phelps-Stokes Fund reasoned that what worked among southern U.S. blacks would work equally well for Africans, and proceeded accordingly. Although criticized by powerful black leaders such as W. E. B. Du Bois, the Jeanes Schools opened the door to a range of African programs for the corporation and reaffirmed the trustees' conviction that the solution to Africa's ills lay in educational development.

Corporation president Frederick Keppel made a study tour of the continent in 1927 and upon his return set aside $500,000 for a five-year survey of the educational needs of British Africa. During the next decade and a half, over $1 million in corporation funds were allocated for Jeanes Schools, research on Africa, and library support in southern, western, and eastern sub-Saharan Africa, programs which helped to whet the corporation's interest in African education and strengthened its commitment to devising projects suited to indigenous development needs.

The program was expanded during the 1950s to include support of African studies programs in the United States and a broader focus to the corporation's efforts in Africa. Following a series of conferences among U.S. and British (and later, African) educators, foundation representatives, and policy makers, a new program was devised which emphasized Anglo-American cooperation, university development, efforts to relate university programs to community needs, and an increased emphasis on African research and library development. Special efforts were also made to generate interest among other U.S. foundations. Cultural projects played a minor role in these early undertakings. Although large humanities grants were occasionally made—for example, Carnegie's $45,000 grant to the University of Ibadan in 1956 for research on West African history—most of the money was spent on educational reform.

The Rockefeller Foundation has evinced a stronger, but still scattered, interest in fostering cultural research in Africa. A 1959 memo outlined the foundation's plan of attack. Noting that "a large part of the continent will soon consist of independent, self-governing nations," Africanist Robert July asserted that "America can make its best contribution to Africa" by aiding the Africans to develop the capabilities necessary for "running successfully the nations they are making." This approach suggested a variety of efforts, ranging from agricultural reform to managerial training. But there were other important aspects which July felt might be neglected, and should not be. As he explained:

Spiritual needs—more difficult to divine, to localize, and to do something about—for the Africans and for us—are relatively ignored in the welter of economic planning, political activity, and public health programs. Yet if men are to be free, to what end is this freedom directed? If life is pointless, is not a longer life more pointless still? There is an equal need for national philosophies to match economic change and social progress and to give them meaning and justification.[4]

July went on to detail a number of possible lines of attack, with history heading the list. "The past must be studied as it never has in Africa," he noted, in order "to show people what they have been, why they are as they are, and where they are going." At that time several promising starts had already been made by the nations themselves. The University of Dakar was in the initial stages of devising an African studies program, and Nigeria's University College had an Islamic studies center on the drawing board. The latter program was deemed particularly important, since "the country is over 50% Muslim and since its further cohesiveness depends to a large extent on the ability of Muslim and non-Muslim population to live together" in harmony.[5] In these newly independent nations, humanistic endeavors could play a potentially significant role.

Other disciplines were singled out as well. Fellowships and

travel grants were recommended for dramatists and writers; art schools were to be encouraged, museums developed, and linguistic programs put into effect. Universities, too, might benefit from the foundation's attention, for "any national solution to Africa's racial problems will have to come through education." New programs should be initiated, and a particular emphasis was to be placed on the Africanization of faculty as the colonial forces withdrew. By the same token, travel grants would help to nurture local talent and contribute to the rise of pan-Africanism. As July explained, "One of the most striking impressions which a traveler receives in Africa is the almost total lack of contact between Africans of different countries," owing, in large measure, to the deliberate policies of the colonial governments. In order to mitigate intellectual and political parochialism in the new nations, efforts would have to be made "to enable Africans representing a wide front of national interests and activities to visit, to live in, to study, and to know other African countries."[6]

The Rockefeller Foundation moved into culturally related activities in Africa in the 1950s, with a particular eye to defining national values and distinguishing African culture from the colonial norms which had dominated society prior to independence. In Ghana, experiments were undertaken in the visual arts and musical forms at the national University College's Institute of African Studies. Other programs were undertaken to foster the writing of African history by Africans themselves, one of the most successful of which was Bethwell Ogot's oral history project at the Institute of African Studies at the University of Nairobi. When the foundation initiated its university development program in 1963 (later renamed Education for Development in the 1970s), a limited humanities component was included in its efforts. At the universities of Ibadan, Makerere, Nairobi, and Dar Es Salaam, the foundation labored to expand curricular offerings, increase library holdings, and Africanize faculties.

History programs were among the primary beneficiaries. With Rockefeller funding, professors at the University of Ibadan developed a joint research project on the history of Benin and a publication program for monographs on African history, and launched a major program in Islamic history, culture, and linguistic studies. A national archive was established for the recovery and preservation of Nigeria's cultural heritage. Promising scholars were granted fellowship funds, and faculty exchanges and visiting fellowships were encouraged. Later the university received a $160,000 grant for its language laboratory. Similar efforts were made at the University of Nairobi, where the Cultural Division of the Institute for Development Studies was launched with Rockefeller funding in 1965. Bethwell Ogot's presence had a considerable effect on the quality of the programs developed at Nairobi. With his aid, anthropologists, linguists, archaeologists, and historians collaborated to devise new methods of deciphering the nation's past through a unique blend of written, oral, and material sources.

Ford also funded selected African humanists as part of its campaign to indigenize national universities, and fostered the expansion of African studies centers in the United States. Although the humanities were never a major component of the foundation's African program, substantial linguistic efforts and similar undertakings were initiated when companionable with the foundation's larger development aims. Language training programs were undertaken in Nigeria and East Africa, including programs to test the efficacy of primary educational curricula taught in vernacular languages such as Yoruba. Smaller sums were also occasionally given for specific cultural undertakings, for example, a $10,000 grant to Wole Soyinka for a cultural survey in 1976, ongoing support for Chinua Achebe's literary journal, *Okike,* and a more recent grant of $7,000 to a Tanzanian publishing house to bring out a Swahili-language historical novel on the nation's precolonial period. But Ford's primary emphasis in Africa has clearly been on social, economic, and managerial development, rather than culture.

U.S. support of Third World humanistic activities has afforded a mixed legacy of failure and success. Certainly, the "welfare colonialism" of the postwar decades drew its share of criticism, as well as praise. In a candid assessment of the Latin American University for Development program which he helped to create, former Rockefeller staffer John P. Harrison noted that the foundation had aimed too high in the humanities. Although university enrollments climbed steadily after World War II, Latin American youths were far more interested in securing technical degrees than in honing humanistic skills. Harrison argued that the foundation's funds might have been better placed had they been used to support small groups of humanists working outside academe, or to develop primary- and secondary-level texts with significant cultural content. Robert July echoed Harrison's findings, noting that funding of individual African scholars rather than university programs might have produced more enduring returns.

In part, this suggestion reflects a growing debate about the relative merits of academic and vocational training in underdeveloped parts of the world. Universities have come under attack for their inherent elitism, their promulgation of Western norms. Based on Western models, instructing students in Western languages, with Western books and often Western faculties as well, Third World universities have come to be viewed by some as citadels for the maintenance and celebration of Western culture at the expense of indigenous needs.

As the initial exhilaration of the first years of independence settled into the more mundane realities of long, slow processes of modernization, maturing governments adopted increasingly "reserved—indeed, sometimes suspicious or truculent—postures toward rich foreigners bearing supposed gifts." In the process, the "easy cooperation that marked the beginnings of international development assistance" was replaced by mutual suspicion and "a rather grumpy maturity."[7] In Ford's case, these events have loosened the foundation's formerly close working relationships with Third World governments and have led to a sharp decline in the number of project specialists in technical-assistance assignments. Rockefeller, too, is currently phasing out its Education for Development programs.

Few other U.S. foundations, and even fewer corporations, have undertaken international humanistic work in the last decade, and the activities of this select pool have been dominated by Rockefeller, the Exxon Education Foundation, Mellon, and Ford. Among the other U.S. foundations currently at work in the international arena, a few supply limited support for the humanities. Since its founding in 1940 by the children of John D. Rockefeller, Jr., the Rockefeller Brothers Fund has devoted a small but significant portion of its budget to foreign activities, including grants for exchanges, translations, and efforts to enhance international cooperation. Similarly, the Luce Foundation and the JDR 3rd Fund foster artistic and cultural exchanges between the United States and Asia, and the Tinker Foundation fulfills the same role for Latin America.

Even among the largest foundations, support for international humanistic work has been a tenuous priority at best. Although the Mellon Foundation encourages domestic programs to enhance international understanding through the humanities, few of its grants have been expended outside the United States. Rockefeller's gifts to non-U.S. humanistic undertakings over the last nine years have been sporadic, at best. The Ford Foundation, which traditionally has donated the lion's share of private funding for international cultural endeavors, has sharply reduced its expenditures since the 1960s. Between 1960 and 1967, Ford's yearly outlays for advanced training and research in international affairs and area studies averaged $27 million; by the late 1970s this figure had fallen to less than $3 million. Federal expenditures for these disciplines have also declined, from $20.3 million in 1969 to $8.5 million in 1978. According to one source, "As a result of these cutbacks, the nation's network of area centers, programs on international problems, schools for advanced studies, libraries, overseas research facilities, and senior research exchange programs . . . was brought to the brink of collapse."[8]

Area studies have received the largest amount of foundation support for domestically based international humanistic endeavors, followed by programs in language training and history. This priority is hardly surprising, for area studies programs have the clearest policy implications among the humanistically oriented international fields, serving governmental and corporate aims while allowing scholars to pursue basic, interdisciplinary research. The figures in Tables 1–4 are only impressionistic, and undoubtedly deceptively high. Owing to the method of foundation reporting, it is impossible to separate social science projects from purely humanistic concerns; area studies are inherently a blend of both. What the tables do suggest is the degree of ongoing foundation interest in this type of work, and patterns of support in the areas of greatest concern (see Table 1 for aggregate figures).

Not surprisingly, Russian, Eastern European, and Asian (particularly Chinese) studies have been well funded in comparison to studies of the more exotic geographic areas (see Table 2). This weighting is clearly a reflection of cold war imperatives and the legacy of détente. Yet even Russian and Asian studies have experienced cyclical funding patterns. One of the most positive trends is that corporate support has been steadily on the rise, owing largely to the contributions of the Exxon Education Foundation.

Yet the data for even this well-funded field reveal potential problems and areas of neglect. Foundation interest in area studies peaked in the mid-1960s and has since steadily declined (see Table 3). In the process, areas such as Africa and the Middle East have

Table 1. AMERICAN FOUNDATION GRANTS FOR INTERNATIONALLY
ORIENTED HUMANITIES PROJECTS IN THE UNITED STATES
1972–1980 FIELDS AND PURPOSES

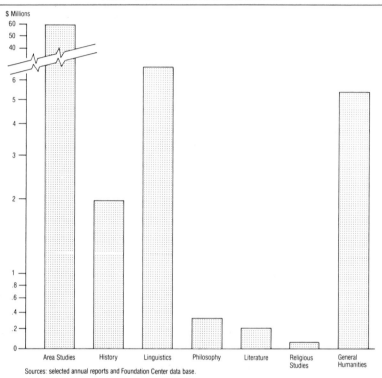

Sources: selected annual reports and Foundation Center data base.

suffered increasing neglect. Ironically, the initial drive to strengthen area studies programs was born of the growing awareness during the Second World War that the United States lacked uniformly strong capabilities for analysis of the rest of the world. Dwindling support for Third World area studies is an unhealthy sign that the nation's scholarly resources concerning nonaligned nations are once again declining, and declining at the precise moment when these countries are having their greatest impact on international policy making.

Linguistic study is closely related to area studies and as such has experienced similar funding trends, including a boom-and-

Table 2. AMERICAN FOUNDATION GRANTS FOR AREA STUDIES
PROGRAMS BASED IN THE UNITED STATES 1972–1980

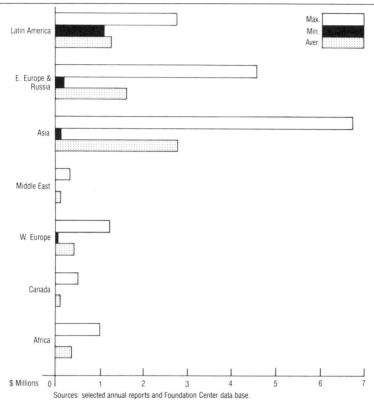

Sources: selected annual reports and Foundation Center data base.

bust cycle of support. Ford played a particularly important role in the development of language programs both at home and abroad, with the Mellon Foundation once again running a respectable second. Here, too, corporate interest has made a significant impact, owing to the efforts of the Exxon Education Foundation. Because adequate language skills are essential for successful multinational marketing, linguistic capabilities can be directly related to company profits, and so this is a particularly appropriate field for corporate support. For example, when advertising campaigns are undertaken without sophisticated knowledge of local customs, idioms,

Table 3. AMERICAN FOUNDATION GRANTS FOR INTERNATIONALLY ORIENTED HUMANITIES PROJECTS IN THE UNITED STATES 1972–1980 SELECTED FIELDS

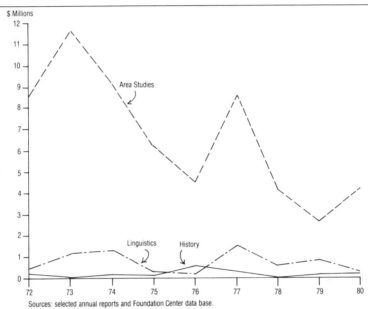

Sources: selected annual reports and Foundation Center data base.

and linguistic usage, the results can be ludicrous. As a recent pamphlet by the National Council on Foreign Language and International Studies points out:

> When General Motors put out its Chevrolet Nova, apparently no one thought of foreign sales. Nova, when spoken as two words in Spanish, means, "It doesn't go." Not surprisingly, sales in Puerto Rico and Latin America were few. "Body by Fisher," describing another General Motors product, translated as "Corpse by Fisher" in Flemish. Schweppes Tonic Water was advertised in Italy as "bathroom water." "Come Alive with Pepsi" nearly appeared in the Chinese version of *Reader's Digest* as "Pepsi Brings Your Ancestors Back from the Grave."[9]

Within universities, Russian- and European-language programs have been the most amply funded, outdistancing those for other areas. Independent research and training centers have also been well supported, particularly the Center for Applied Linguistics, which has netted a healthy $2,615,000 over the past nine years.

History, another key discipline in area studies work, has been generously funded. The bulk of this money, which has remained fairly constant over the course of the last decade, has gone into research, conferences, and institutional development. It should also be mentioned that substantial numbers of historians and other humanists, including those pursuing topics of international interest, are funded through the fellowship competitions of the Rockefeller and Guggenheim foundations, the American Council of Learned Societies, the Social Science Research Council, and the National Endowment for the Humanities. The Ford Foundation developed an additional humanities fellowship competition in 1981, but discontinued the program the following year.

Support for humanists of all disciplines has been made available through grants for conferences, fellowships, and research through the American Council of Learned Societies, the Social Science Research Council, and the International Research and Exchanges Board, but specific disciplinary areas other than history have not fared well. Only Rockefeller has consistently spread its support across all fields in the humanities. Philosophy, literature, religious studies—all have received short shrift in the overall funding picture.

Within the international arena, the Ford Foundation has clearly dominated the scene, aided by its field officers throughout the world who select and monitor grants on an ongoing basis. Ford's interest is largely due to its ongoing commitment to the role of scholarly activities as part of its larger development schemes and to its cultural preservation work in Asia, which appears to be on the upswing. Between January and July of 1982 alone, over $600,000 was spent on cultural activities via the foundation's Asian and Pacific outposts. Recent grants in this area include an allocation of $175,000 for the development of ethnomusicology in Indonesia, $88,000 for a program in folk performing arts in India, and $200,000 to foster creative writing in Indian regional languages.

The largest numbers of foreign-based humanities grants have been expended in Europe and Asia, with the rest of the world falling significantly behind (see Table 4). Some of these allocations have been made as part of a specific programmatic thrust,

Table 4. AMERICAN FOUNDATION GRANTS FOR HUMANITIES PROJECTS IN FOREIGN COUNTRIES 1972–1980 RECIPIENT AREAS AND PURPOSES

	Language Study & Education	Research	Universities & Centers	Translations & Publications	Area Studies	Conferences	Cultural Preservation	Archival & Library Development	Fellowships	Total	
Africa	$ 1,280,000	$ 25,000	$ 82,000	$ 205,000	$	$	$ 104,000	$ 200,000	$	$1,896,000	7.7%
Asia and Pacific	3,573,000	575,000		33,000	798,000	26,000	8,134,000	78,000		13,217,000	53.9%
Europe	315,000	1,069,000	3,000,000	189,000	778,000	48,000		267,000	2,175,000	6,091,000	24.8%
Middle East & N Africa	1,566,000	200,000		113,000	102,000			76,000		2,057,000	8.4%
Latin America & Caribbean	361,000	400,000	219,000	178,000					121,000	1,279,000	5.2%
										24,540,000	100%

Sources: selected annual reports and Foundation Center data base.

such as the Rockefeller Foundation's work with faculty development in Latin America. Other grants have been made in a more casual way, in response to "over-the-transom" requests. However, the contributions of Rockefeller and Ford are not typical of most American foundation grants, for the vast majority of the nation's foundations still confine their activities to domestic programs which exclude the humanities. As former Council on Foundations chairman Landrum Bolling points out, there is currently "no grand strategy of foundation involvement in international affairs, no agreement on the importance of private support for international activities, no broadly shared sense of priorities for American philanthropic giving related to international interests."[10]

Although humanistic support from the leading private foundations is likely to continue at somewhat the same level, the corporate prognosis is less clear. Corporate foundation outlays now surpass private foundation giving, a trend which may ultimately generate new types of philanthropic alliances in the United States. Spending by private foundations has hovered between $2 billion and $3 billion over the last decade, signaling a significant decline in real purchasing power, while corporate contributions and social investments have been on the upswing and may continue to rise in the next decade.

As the movement for corporate social responsibility gains momentum, the opportunities for expansion seem almost limitless. Congress recently raised the ceiling on tax-deductible corporate gifts from 5 percent to 10 percent of pretax net income. What this change will mean for international philanthropy, or for the humanities, remains to be seen. At present, corporate interest in both areas is muted at best. The 1980 statistics of the Conference Board, which annually surveys the scope and breadth of corporate philanthropy, reveal that of 732 companies, donations of those making gifts to organizations aiding other countries totaled $17.4 million, or 1.7 percent of the survey's total corporate gifts. These figures are, of course, merely rough estimates, since much international corporate giving is distributed through foreign offices, rather than from within the United States. Nevertheless, the competing demands of domestic concerns, the difficulty of monitoring overseas grants with limited staffs, and the sheer weight of tradition will undoubtedly militate against the expansion of corporate foreign aid.

Business support of the humanities has traditionally been

tentative at best. Although a few corporations make donations to established organizations like the American Council of Learned Societies and cooperate with private foundations on collaborative undertakings like the Research Libraries Group, they are in the minority. However, a handful of American companies have recently taken the lead in developing innovative international humanistic programs of their own. For example, the Mobil Corporation created the Pegasus Prize for Literature in 1977, to provide international recognition for talented authors writing in languages other than English. Winners receive $1,000, and their works are translated into English for publication by the Louisiana State University Press. Candidates are nominated from the countries in which Mobil operates, and the company thus conforms to the standard practice of confining grants to bases of corporate activity. A program such as this benefits the company, the reading public, and the humanities at one and the same time. But projects of this nature are clearly in the minority.

As Robert Payton of the Exxon Education Foundation explains, what is needed now is a more sophisticated level of dialogue between humanists and corporate donors, along with more vigorous efforts to explore areas of mutual concern: "The self-interest of the businessman is to understand the social forces that so powerfully affect the environment within which he does business. The self-interest of the academic is to find patrons, sources of support beyond the marketplace and legislature that will enable him to pursue his ideas wherever they may lead—and in the process enlighten engineers and accountants as well as fellow scholars." Business should support humanistic inquiry, according to Payton, because "ideas have consequences . . . and some of the most powerful forces at work today in our society and in the world are products of the humanities and the social sciences distilled over very long periods of time." Language study, philosophical inquiries into ethical issues in the United States and abroad, writing programs—all have relevance for the corporate community. Updating C. P. Snow's "two cultures," Payton concludes, "The two cultures today pit a businessman uninformed about justice against a literary humanist uninformed about profit."[11]

Scholarship, outreach programs, cultural preservation activities, institutional development, translation schemes—opportunities for new and original programs exist on every level, as do reasons for the creation and implementation of such programs at home and abroad. As John D. Rockefeller 3rd noted, Americans have traditionally tended to view international relations "primarily in political and economic terms with comparatively little attention given to the cultural dimension," with the result that "our world outlook has tended to be bound by our own culture instead of being broadened by sensitivity to other cultures; this remains largely so today."[12] Foundation veterans have also noted that foreign educational programs have often been "too instrumental, too much the way to a job and a better income, rather than a source of illumination and personal resource in everyday life."[13] After two decades of development assistance, developers "have begun to sense the cost of progress . . . [as] the sterile discipline of western industrialization displaces centuries of tradition. Cultural heritages are trampled in the march toward the future. . . . The developers have begun to realize that a nation cannot survive on economics alone."[14]

Despite the obvious benefits, the future of American foundation support for national and international humanistic concerns remains unclear. With the possible exception of Soviet studies, support for area studies and linguistic scholarship peaked in the early and mid-1960s, and grants to foreign recipients have echoed the same pattern. As the massive programs of the postwar years are phased out, they will be replaced by new, as yet undefined, aims. Governmental cutbacks have given domestic claims added authority, possibly to the detriment of international work. With the exception of a few outstanding donors such as the Exxon Education Foundation, corporate funding, which may assume an increasing share of philanthropic responsibility in the coming decades, seems destined to have little impact on international cultural concerns. The 1980s promise to be a period of reassessment and flux in the structure of American philanthropy and the state of support for humanistic endeavors.

NOTES

1. Melvin J. Fox, *Language Education in Developing Countries: The Changing Role of the Ford Foundation* (Remarks adapted from a statement prepared for ALSED Roundtable, UNESCO, May 1974; reprint, New York: Ford Foundation, n.d.), pp. 7–8.
2. Robert A. Mayer, *Archives in Developing Countries: The Role of*

Private Foundations (Paper delivered at the annual meeting of the Society of American Archivists, 1971; reprint, New York: Ford Foundation, n.d.), p. 6.

3. Quoted in David Carroll, *Chinua Achebe* (New York: Twayne Publishers, 1970), p. ii.

4. Robert July, "Humanities Program in Africa," Rockefeller Foundation memo, July 24, 1959, p. 1, Rockefeller Foundation Files, New York, N.Y.

5. Ibid., pp. 2, 4.

6. Ibid., pp. 16, 11, 12.

7. Francis X. Sutton, *American Foundations and Public Management in Developing Countries* (New York: Ford Foundation, 1977), p. 14.

8. The National Council on Foreign Language and International Studies, untitled pamphlet (n.p., n.d.).

9. Paul Simon, *The Tongue Tied American* (1980), quoted in ibid.

10. Landrum R. Bolling, *Excerpts from "Private Foreign Aid: U.S. Philanthropy for Relief and Development"* (Washington, D.C.: Council on Foundations, 1981), p. 4.

11. Robert L. Payton, "Should Business Support the Humanities?" (Remarks to the Board of Overseers of the Faculty of Arts and Sciences, University of Pennsylvania, March 29, 1982), pp. 5–8.

12. John D. Rockefeller 3rd, Foreword to *The JDR 3rd Fund in Asia, 1963–1975* (New York: JDR 3rd Fund, 1977), p. 8.

13. Francis X. Sutton, "Cultural Implications of Aid Programs" (Paper delivered at the Truman International Conference on Technical Assistance and Development, Hebrew University, Jerusalem, May 1970), p. 14.

14. Mayer, *Archives in Developing Countries,* p. 5.

2 / The Humanities and International Understanding: Some Reflections on the Experience of the Rockefeller Foundation

MALCOLM RICHARDSON

The Rockefeller Foundation has traditionally been one of the most active promoters of the humanities. As the following essay explains, the foundation's commitment to these disciplines was an outgrowth of the officers' larger interest in the promotion of international understanding and interchange. Malcolm Richardson skillfully delineates the foundation's activities, noting the course of changing programmatic priorities, and discusses how the humanities have served as a lightning rod for foundation critics. In the process, he provides an excellent case study of the humanities programs of one of the nation's oldest and largest foundations.

From the outset the Rockefeller Foundation has had an ambitious, almost presumptuous, mandate to "promote the well-being of mankind throughout the world," an injunction which was at first taken literally by its officials, who shaped the foundation's early programs almost exclusively around medical education and public health. With the exception of a large grant to the American Academy in Rome in 1913, the year in which the foundation was created, it took no interest in the humanities until after the First World War.[1]

When the humanities first came to be considered at the Rockefeller offices as a possible field of interest, they were inextricably linked to international affairs. Raymond Fosdick, a trustee of the foundation who had briefly served as an undersecretary at the League of Nations before the Senate vetoed U.S. entry, deserves much of the credit for successfully wresting some portion of the Rockefeller funds from the doctors and broadening the definition of human well-being to include the humanities and fine arts. As the attorney and intimate friend of John D. Rockefeller, Jr.—or at least as intimate a friend as the austere younger Rockefeller permitted himself—Fosdick wielded a quiet but effective influence on the various Rockefeller philanthropies.[2] Convinced that international relations might determine future welfare as much as any other factor, Fosdick spoke and wrote tirelessly on the need for better international understanding. In the early 1920s Rockefeller was thus persuaded to give several million dollars to the League and its affiliates in Geneva. In addition to the much-publicized gift for the library of the League at Geneva, the Rockefeller heir gave substantial sums for League inquiries into the opium trade, "white slavery," and similar social issues under study by League affiliates. At one point as much as half the funds for the League's special projects were supplied by the U.S. millionaire; it is possible that Rockefeller would have agreed to give more had not the secretariat feared charges of undue American influence.[3]

At the same time Fosdick and his colleagues launched an ambitious search for ways to work with European internationalists and the League. The humanities and the social sciences were seen, in effect, as two wings of a broader attack on the problems of creating international understanding and stable institutions in a world still bitterly divided by nationalism and a stubborn parochialism. Every Rockefeller fund was expected to work toward this internationalist cause, including the foundation's operations in public health. Fosdick and the trustees hoped that the public health division, by its neutrality, would serve as an object lesson in the potential benefits of international cooperation. But beyond the contributions to the League and the mobilization of American doctors for international work in medical education, the Rockefeller group thought that more could be done to promote international understanding. Through a form of quiet diplomacy the Rockefeller Foundation and a smaller affiliate, the Laura Spelman Rockefeller Memorial, sought to reinforce European peace groups and to fund a network of centers devoted to maintaining intellectual cooperation. While the foundation worked to build European medical and scientific cooperation, the memorial joined its better-known ally, the Carnegie Endowment for International Peace, in supporting important research centers for the study of international affairs. In particular, the memorial looked for new and potentially influential institutes, funding such research institutions as the Ecole libre de science politique in Paris and the Deutsche Hochschule für Politik in Berlin. When the memorial was absorbed by the foundation, the latter continued to fund these major institutes; likewise, first the memorial and then the foundation aided the efforts of a group of Scandinavian historians to revise European textbooks by eliminating partisan interpretations of the origins of recent wars.

To say that the humanities were expected to contribute to international understanding is to give but one of the reasons for their inclusion in a foundation devoted to the "well-being of mankind." Before considering these other factors, it might be useful to recall the role that the general-purpose foundation was gradually coming to play in an era when the U.S. federal government took no responsibility for education. Not the least of the benefits that were derived from the European studies commissioned by the memorial or other Rockefeller offices was the clearer perception they gave foundation officials of the essential differences between European and U.S. educational systems. As part of a famous survey of civic education in Europe the memorial had sent historian Carlton J. H. Hayes to France. "No country in the world has a more highly centralized system of national education than France," Hayes reported, yet in the same breath he noted admiringly that this centralized system, though in some respects the antithesis of the U.S. ideal, achieved some important results which might be envied by other democracies. Not only did he praise the care and thoroughness with which the entire French curriculum was planned, Hayes thought it probable "that the French system, at least in the past, has operated far more efficiently than the Anglo-American to exalt the position of artists and scholars and to promote the esthetic accomplishment of the few and the esthetic appreciation of the masses."[4] In a federal system with no central governmental responsibility for education, the U.S. foundations—particularly the Carnegie and Rockefeller funds—gave what little central direction or coordination the U.S. system had.[5] Should they not, therefore, encourage a broader diffusion of the arts and humanities?

When considering their responsibilities, the Rockefeller trustees found persuasive several of the arguments advanced on behalf of the humanities. In addition to their role as an antidote to a narrow, technical education and to the pronounced American tendency toward vocationalism, the humanities were seen in broader terms as an essential balance to the paralyzing tendency of scientific skepticism to suspend all esthetic and moral judgment. If science was an international inquiry, and if rapid communications were rendering a narrow partriotism or nationalism obsolete, it was also apparent in the aftermath of the Great War that such progress was far from inevitable or automatic. "With the same hand science gives us X-rays and machine guns, modern surgery and high explosives, anaesthetics and poison gas," Fosdick wrote. "In brief, science has multiplied man's physical powers ten thousand fold and in like ratio has increased his capacity both for construction and destruction. How is that capacity to be used in the future?"[6] The answers to such questions, the trustees thought, had to come from values outside science.

To a certain extent this understanding of the foundation's role and the definition of the humanities given by Fosdick and others implied a criticism of the existing approach to the humanities. As might be expected, Fosdick was a tireless advocate of revising the curriculum to include the newer social sciences and humanistic courses which emphasized modern languages and contemporary studies. Critical of the university's preference for the remote past and the historical approach to philosophy and literature, Fosdick did not think this retreat from responsibility an exclusively American failing. Writing with the Great War's horrors etched on his memory—in one of his published letters Fosdick confessed to his father that nearly two years after the war he often could not sleep at night, troubled by the recollection of what he had seen at the front as a civilian volunteer—he demanded to know what could be said of a traditional education if "Poincaré graduated with high honours from the University of Paris; [if] Sazonov was a distinguished student at the Alexandrovsky Lycee; Bethmann-Hollweg studied at the universities of Strassburg, Leipzig, and Berlin; and Lord Grey graduated from Balliol College, Oxford?"[7]

Despite this brave rhetoric the foundation's program in the humanities began with rather traditional subjects. Contributions to endowments and large research funds for selected U.S. universities were soon followed by a program for aiding libraries and support for U.S. archaeological expeditions. The Rockefeller Foundation appropriated large annual subsidies to the American Council of Learned Societies (ACLS), the principal coordinating agency for the humanities in the United States. Abroad, it aided the great national research libraries in Paris, Berlin, and London and helped Cambridge and Oxford renovate their libraries. Through the American Library Association the foundation's funds aided a number of Latin American libraries to train librarians and archivists.

As helpful as these programs undoubtedly were in linking scholars and readers, they failed to satisfy the trustees entirely. Beginning in 1934 the trustees demanded a more ambitious program which aimed broadly at reaching a wider public audience through the theater and the new media of film and radio; which would actively recruit and train younger scholars in international relations, and especially in areas such as East Asia and Latin America that were deemed neglected by the universities but of critical importance to the United States; and which would accordingly promote language and area studies for Latin America, China, Japan, and, soon after, Russia and East Europe. All of these programs tended to create new corps of teachers and new courses which the universities absorbed rather quickly despite their restricted financial outlook in the midst of the Great Depression.

In so broad a program there were inevitable tensions between the private realm of the humanistic scholar and the public mission given the humanities, between local needs and the international calling of the foundation. These tensions were best reconciled in the foundation's support of language studies and international communication. As it evolved from the trustees' mandate, the program in language study came to have two faces. The first goal was to increase U.S. understanding of non-European cultures and to encourage study of such important but infrequently studied languages as Chinese, Japanese, Russian, and (later) Turkish and Arabic—the "unusual" languages, as one foundation report called them. A second goal came to be the encouragement of auxiliary languages, or second languages, as a way to facilitate better international communication. Janus-like, the foundation's program looked inward and outward at the same time: At home it smiled on the efforts of Americans to learn new languages, while encouraging the study of English abroad.

Prior to 1945 the humanities program in its work in international understanding placed the emphasis on the study of language; after the war, roughly speaking, the emphasis gradually shifted away from this approach, rooted firmly in the humanities, to an interdisciplinary one which created area studies centers and reoriented the work of the foundation in both the humanities and the social sciences away from a European-American axis. "An important emphasis," as Dean Rusk explained the new program to the trustees in 1953, "would be upon increased understanding between Western and non-Western cultures, not merely between the United States and other nations."[8] Entire regions, even continents, suddenly cried out for explanation or interpretation; the humanities, though expected to contribute to the emerging area studies programs, were no longer the dominant partner. Faith in the area studies approach, with its heavy emphasis on contemporary problems in economics and politics, became as close to a dogma as the foundation would permit. At the same time this approach often entailed much criticism of the older approach of the humanistic disciplines. A purely literary and historical education, the new dogma ran, was no longer adequate for international understanding. In keeping with the new spirit, the Rockefeller Foundation stunned its traditional friends in the humanities by ending its annual subsidies to the ACLS.

If the humanities failed to hold their former place, was it not, however, because the traditional approach failed to explain much that was of interest in the postwar world? David Stevens, the director of the foundation's programs in the humanities from 1932 to 1949, saw clearly the limitations of the older education. "Long before the Second World War," he wrote, "it was obvious that the neglect in American scholarship of the major world culture areas outside of Western Europe kept poor our humanism, weakened our diplomacy, and jeopardized our effective participation in world organization."[9] The Rockefeller Foundation's efforts to develop the "unusual" languages had been an important first step in broadening the curriculum and the American outlook; parallel to its work in East Asian languages, the foundation had also worked to improve Latin American and Russian studies by training a generation of language scholars in each area. In a sense, the shift toward area studies programs represented a second stage in the development of a corps of experts on each area, and the new programs were in some ways the logical outcome of the earlier emphasis on neglected languages.

In the decade and a half from 1945 to 1960 the Rockefeller Foundation joined the Ford Foundation and the Carnegie Corporation in supporting the establishment of a number of important new research centers devoted to Southeast Asia, South Asia, the Middle East, and sub-Saharan Africa. "The basic concept of area studies," as Stevens's successor, Burton Fahs, explained, "is the application of many or all of the social sciences and humanistic disciplines . . . toward a better understanding of a single region, well defined in both time and geography."[10] Without giving its previous subsidies to the ACLS and the traditional disciplines, the foundation nonetheless continued to support a program in humanistic research; between 1950 and 1960 it found its budget ample enough to fund a fairly flexible program of scholarly research in history, linguistics, and philosophy, loosely grouped around the general theme of "intercultural understanding." Dogma aside, the approach to the humanities was highly flexible.

Looking back at these years from a period of inflated dollars, tightened budgets, and (at least at the Rockefeller Foundation) more rigidly structured programs, the freedom and flexibility with which this earlier approach operated seems almost idyllic. By the mid-1950s the foundation was running a variety of programs grouped loosely around the central idea of interpreting one culture to another. This premise made it possible, if not necessary, to create the counterpart of the area studies center abroad; the foundation accordingly funded a number of American studies programs in Japan, Europe, and Turkey. Finally, the Rockefeller Foundation overcame a long-standing reluctance to fund artists and writers; once it broadened its definition of the humanities to include creative writing, the foundation funded fellowships for writers in Great Britain from 1947 to 1950 (the Atlantic Awards), in Canada (via the Canada Foundation), in Mexico from 1951 to the mid-1960s at the Mexican Center for Writers, and in Nigeria through fellowships and the drama department at the University of Ibadan.

The foundation, on occasion, even broke its own rules against providing operating expenses to magazines or performing arts groups. In 1960, for example, it funded the tour of a Japanese Kabuki troupe in order to make possible a new type of theatrical experience for U.S. audiences. In general, some idea of the flexibility or leeway given officers can be gathered from an article Burton Fahs contributed to a Japan Foundation publication:

In my years with the Rockefeller Foundation I was fortunate in that I could recommend fellowships for students from any country to any country or to two or more countries. I did, for example, enable Japanese to study in India and Turkey. Dr. Lie Tek Tjeng, now one of Indonesia's leading experts on Asia, was first enabled to go to the United States on a one-year Fulbright grant. When that expired, the Rockefeller Foundation enabled him to study in Japan and also to return to Harvard to complete his doctorate. Study in both countries was, I think, essential to his development as a scholar and statesman. Each of the Japanese writers to whom we gave fellowships was offered the opportunity to spend half the fellowship period in a country or countries other than the United States. Thus Fukuda Tsuneari went to England because of his interest in T. S. Eliot and there also fell in love with Shakespeare and drama. Ooka Shohei, who had been a Stendhal expert, followed that author's peregrinations in France and Italy. When we gave a few grants for study in the United States to Indonesian labor leaders, we enabled them to stop in the Philippines or Japan en route to the United States to establish contact with labor leaders there. We let them visit Europe, and, if they were Muslims, Mecca on their way home.[11]

Whether sending Muslims via Mecca or Indonesians via Japan, Fahs wanted to avoid restricting fellowships and exchanges to bilateral channels. By emancipating itself from the artificial limits of two-party exchanges, the foundation managed to take a longer view of U.S. interests and to allay suspicions that the foundation worked to promote only those interests. Persuaded that the study of East Asia would benefit from many different centers of excellence, Fahs did not hesitate to offer major support to the Toyo Bunko, a major Japanese research center with important resources for the study of China, and to develop Indonesian centers for the study of Japan.

From time to time the foundation also took an interest in translation projects. Two such experiments might be mentioned in passing. In the late 1950s the humanities officers launched two ambitious series, one designed to translate European and American classics into Arabic, a project which was eventually taken up by another sponsor, and a highly successful plan to translate Latin American literary and historical works into English. In the latter plan the Rockefeller Foundation offered subsidies to a consortium of U.S. university presses to pay translation costs and incidental scholarly expenses. With agreement in advance from the editors, from the translators and scholars, and from the foundation, it was possible to choose a carefully planned list of books which covered the history and culture of Latin America from colonial times to the recent past. This small library of translated works would have been a useful contribution to many college and public libraries, but the major impact of this translation series probably came in the expanded appreciation of contemporary South American literature which followed. Among the contemporary writers whose works of fiction or poetry were translated were such now-familiar names as Jorge Luis Borges, Octavio Paz, and Carlos Fuentes. Designed in part to attract commercial publishers to such editions, this modest program seems in retrospect to have worked beyond all expectation.

As always, the tug between local needs and international appeals for aid forced difficult decisions. By 1962 the Rockefeller Foundation seems to have felt that its previous budgets, with their generous provisions for supporting the arts and humanities within the United States, had accomplished their original purpose. The United States had well-staffed research centers for every major cultural area and sufficient resources to support them. With some justice the foundation also observed in 1962, when it merged the social sciences and humanities into one administrative unit, that "these two programs had often overlapped" and that "their separation became more and more artificial."[12] By consolidating these programs and reducing the funds appropriated for the humanities at home, the foundation could revise its budget to free important sums for aiding universities in the developing countries.

In addition to these internal considerations, it should be mentioned that there were important external factors too. In 1958 Congress had provided large federal subsidies for area studies centers and for language training through the National Defense Education Act. A few years later the creation of the National Endowment for the Humanities extended government funding throughout the humanities and eliminated other claims on the foundation's budget. Not long after the establishment of this federal agency for the humanities, the officers at the Rockefeller Foundation were no longer asking what role they might play in the humanities but asking "whether there is a continuing role for this Foundation in the humanities."[13]

Forced to choose between programs which seemed destined to receive federal funds and the unmet needs in the developing nations, the foundation gave its highest priority to training new cadres of technicians, agronomists, and doctors. The strategy chosen in 1962 emphasized the development of universities in key centers in Latin America, Africa, and Asia; this approach had much to recommend it, given the limited resources of the foundation and the huge needs in the developing countries. Foundation support, as the annual report which announced this new emphasis admitted, had to be "highly selective, concentrating on a small number of institutions with the greatest potential for national and international distinction."[14] While the strengthening of humanities and social science faculties may not have held the highest priority in this new program of university development, they were not entirely forgotten, and within the budgets of each of the selected universities there were significant sums for fellowships, for recruiting visiting U.S. professors, and for books and other research needs. Yet, as far as the humanities were concerned, a tacit assumption in this new program was that institutional development—as opposed to more dispersed searches for individual talent—was as necessary or as constructive in the humanities as it patently was for the more expensive and capital-intensive programs in science and medicine. The freewheeling days when the Rockefeller Foundation was funding translation projects, indigenous drama in Nigeria, creative writing in Mexico, and the like suddenly came to an end.

Although the humanities did in fact continue to figure in the Rockefeller Foundation's programs at home and abroad, from 1962 to 1971 its spending for them dropped precipitously. By its own accounting in the years from 1963 to 1968 spending for the humanities outside the framework of the university development projects totaled hardly more than $700,000.[15] By contrast, from 1950 to 1962 the humanities budget was never less than $1 million in any one year and often ran as high as $3 or $4 million. Once regarded as essential to international intercourse, the humanities had somehow become marginal even to the foundation which had supported them longest.

The foundation's current program in the humanities began in the conviction that the really important questions facing the world in the last quarter of the century are neither quantitative nor entirely factual, but involve hard choices among conflicting values. Once again, the humanities are seen as indispensable, not because they provide immediate answers but because they provide the only framework of inquiry in which such questions as the nature of international obligations, of human rights and economic justice, and of basic national purposes can be answered intelligently.

At the same time, when the trustees reemphasized the humanities in 1974, there were abundant signs that U.S. society and its schools needed such leadership. In the same spirit the foundation's own Commission on the Humanities concluded that a "dramatic improvement in the quality of education in our elementary and secondary schools is the highest educational priority for America in the 1980's"[16] and suggested that only with a greater emphasis on languages, literature, philosophy, and history could this objective be achieved.

Even before the Rockefeller Foundation's panel brought in its verdict in 1980, a national commission appointed by President Carter had delivered an even more strongly worded warning about the decline of the humanities. The Perkins Commission, to use its journalistic nickname, described U.S. teaching in foreign languages and area studies as a matter of "scandalous incompetence" and convincingly tied U.S. political and diplomatic embarrassments to this educational failure. The commission worried aloud that such intellectual lassitude might also mean a growing inability to compete in world markets:

> Our schools graduate a large majority of students whose knowledge and vision stops at the American shoreline, whose approach to international affairs is provincial, and whose heads have been filled with astonishing misinformation. In a recently published study of school children's knowledge and perceptions of other nations and peoples, over 40 per cent of the 12th graders could not locate Egypt correctly, while over 20 per cent were equally ignorant about the whereabouts of France or China. At the college level, an American Council on Education study reported that at most only 5 per cent of prospective teachers take any course relating to international affairs or foreign peoples and cultures as part of their professional preparation. A 1977 Gallup Poll furthermore showed that those who graduate from an educational system so glaringly deficient in this vital area carry their ignorance with them into their adult lives: over half of the general public was unaware that the United States must import part of its petroleum supplies.

Finally, the Perkins Commission reported that it found among both educators and government officials a "complacent and defeatist attitude" that nothing effective would or could be done.[17] As overstated as one suspects that this indictment is, could there be a clearer case for the need for an intensified commitment to the humanities?

It might be wondered how such a dearth of learning could prevail in an educational system so abundantly funded by state and local sources, by private foundations, and from 1958 until very recently, by ever-increasing increments from the federal government. No single explanation will suffice, but it may be appropriate to ask what role U.S. foundations have played. Can the foundations, after claiming a leadership role in the American system, escape part of the blame?

For all their accomplishments, American philanthropies have had their critics, and the complaints of the more responsible among them have a particular relevance to a conference dealing with the humanities. Abraham Flexner, who lent his hand to the creation of the Rockefeller Foundation's first programs in the humanities, argued in 1952 that no U.S. foundation had taken the humanities seriously. In retrospect it might be thought that the Rockefeller Foundation's annual subsidies to the ACLS, its decisive support for the graduate programs in the "unusual" languages, and its early support for area studies might have exempted it from Flexner's scorn. In fairness, Flexner might also have noted the work of the Guggenheim Foundation or the Carnegie Corporation, the latter of which, if it did not maintain professional staffs or divisions exclusively devoted to the humanities, nonetheless funded a number of programs in art appreciation, in adult education, and in museum and library work of great importance to the humanities. Yet in an indictment entitled "The Neglect of the Humanities," a crime of which a great many U.S. philanthropies were certainly guilty, Flexner argued that the failure of U.S. foundations to understand the reciprocal relationship between the humanities and the sciences endangered the entire educational system. Nothing proved the failure of foundation leadership—another of Flexner's charges—better than the one-sided pattern of their expenditures. Calling the humanities "the crying need of modern America," Flexner thought "a judicious critic would probably maintain that humanism has fairly well held its own in Great Britain and on the Continent, but in the United States has fought a losing battle."[18]

The case against foundations has also been strongly argued, from the 1950s to the present, by another distinguished American humanist, Jacques Barzun, who insists that the long-term effect of foundation giving has been to undermine the humanities. Attacking with wit what he terms the "principle of compulsory newness," Barzun has pilloried the subtle condescension which he finds to be the hallmark of foundation-university relations. "No one engaged in the central duties of a going concern could be foundation fodder," Barzun wrote, "but obviously, any such persons should be encouraged to take a look at his performance, in the expectation that when he saw it as it really was he would do something else." The tendency of the foundations to emphasize innovation at the expense of tradition inevitably put the humanities at a disadvantage. "The humanities gave rise to no projects, properly so called, were not expensive enough, and promised few social benefits," Barzun explained. "Their work remained invisible. To support it was like gambling sums too small to be exciting, on horses altogether too dark."[19]

Barzun's indictment goes further, however. Beyond the fate of the humanities in and of themselves, he maintains that U.S. colleges and universities have been damaged, and that the fate of the larger intellectual enterprise is not unrelated to the ills of the humanities. The emphasis on research and on useful studies with measurable results has betrayed a misconception not only of the humanities but of the entire university. Yet since it is plainly easier to base tenure and promotion decisions, to say nothing of pay differentials, on the more visible record of research and publication than on the less tangible qualities of intellect and teaching, administrators have come to regard the foundation grant or fellowship as a sign of grace. The foundation grant, according to its critics, has thus introduced a subtle corruption into academic life, driving a wedge between teaching and research. Let Barzun speak for himself:

> The effect of foundation grants on our seats of learning has been simple and may be shortly stated: inflation and strain. By pouring money into projects, studies, and institutes—all new and superimposed on existing purposes—the foundations have steadily added to the financial and administrative burdens of universities, while creating on the rim of the central structure vested interests whose allegiance is to the outside source of funds, not to the institution they happen to belong to. The unity and sense of loyalty of large companies of scholars have thus been undermined.

Or, in sum, "by baited gifts, the foundations have insidiously impoverished university teaching."[20]

This tendency to emphasize immediate social benefits can also be linked to the ascendancy of the social sciences. Both Barzun and Flexner scored the preference of foundations for the social sciences over the humanities. The Rockefeller Foundation has indeed been something of a barometer, as historian John Higham has noticed, in measuring the rising or falling pressures of the social sciences on the humanities and vice versa. The foundation's decision to create both a division for the social sciences and a separate one for the humanities during its reorganization in 1928–29, Higham suggested, hardened a crippling cleavage in the American mind. "In a rough way it might be said that Europeans distinguish principally between natural science and the study of man, whereas Americans are more likely to draw a sharp boundary between 'science' of every sort and the 'humanities.' "[21]

In the United States both universities and foundations, Higham decided, drafted "a somewhat distinctive map of the geography of high culture on which social sciences and humanities appear as rival confederations disputing territory they jointly occupy." Although Higham conceded in his survey of U.S. scholarship that this specialization had without doubt forwarded some fields, his final verdict was, on balance, quite harsh: "Consequently, we have too little 'art' in one camp, too little 'science' in the other, and not enough breadth of mind in either."[22] In this view foundations do not bear all the guilt; far from creating this characteristic failing of American intellectual life, the foundations merely ratified or perpetuated it.

In fairness to the foundations, quite a few of their officers understood the narrowness of vision imposed by single-minded research in any one field of specialization. In fact, foundation support for area studies might be explained, at least in part, by their power to focus or unite many separate disciplines in a common effort to understand a given culture. Area studies seemed at one point to be the magic elixir which might unite the disciplines and cure the schizophrenic U.S. curriculum. "What is required is the restructuring of intellectual and research concerns on an unprecedented scale," Burton Fahs wrote in 1954 in one internal critique of the Rockefeller Foundation's work in area studies. "The educational problems of the world era now upon us cannot be met merely by superimposing new courses or institutes but will require rethinking of curricula in ways which perhaps cannot now be foreseen. It is entirely reasonable that such a development should require much more than twenty years."[23]

Nearly thirty years have elapsed since Fahs wrote his prescription for integrating international studies into the curriculum, but it seems safe to conclude—as the Perkins Commission bears eloquent witness—that we in the United States are no closer to balancing the demands of a new era with the claims of educational tradition. Still, Flexner and Barzun notwithstanding, it also seems clear that the private foundations in the United States have done reasonably well in encouraging advanced research and in assisting colleges and universities with programs that they, the universities, have chosen.

Reflecting on the experience of the Rockefeller Foundation, one is struck by how well foundations can do certain things—arrange a timely conference, offer flexible fellowships or study grants, make available skilled professionals for developing nations, or underwrite translation ventures—with a minimum of red tape and delay. Yet, to judge only from the experience of the Rockefeller Foundation, they have done less well in figuring out how the fruits of these international exchanges might be shared with a larger public. If even half of the indictment in the report of the Perkins Commission is true of U.S. schools, the gap decried over fifty years ago by the Rockefeller trustees between the public's knowledge and its leaders' responsibilities does not seem to have grown any smaller but may be, if anything, wider.

At the same time the stakes in international communication have seldom been higher. It is nonetheless probable that in a climate of retrenchment, not only in the United States but in many industrial nations, the humanities will be among the first casualties in the curtailment of government and private budgets. When public and private funds are under such strains, the humanities are vulnerable to exactly the kinds of pressures diagnosed by Flexner and Barzun. In competition with the sciences and social needs, the humanities in the short run seem to have less to offer. As representatives of a constituency clamoring for its share of scarce resources, the spokespersons for the humanities are relatively weak in numbers and shy in public forums. In such circumstances it would seem that foundations do have a real, if restricted, role to play as advocates arguing for the priority of the humanities.

David Stevens, the director for the humanities mentioned earlier, liked to quote George Sarton on this latter point, and Sarton's dictum can hardly be improved upon. "The humanities," he wrote, "are not useful, but they are necessary."[24] The discovery of how essential the humanities are to any broadly conceived plan for promoting international understanding perhaps explains why, no matter how often they have been abandoned or deemphasized, the Rockefeller Foundation has found it necessary to revive the humanities as a program emphasis. For any real understanding between nations, and not only in the sense of diplomatic entente but in the deeper sense of mutual comprehension and respect, the study of language, literature, philosophy, and history is essential.

Finally, to assert that the humanities are essential for a foundation which works internationally is not to claim that internationally oriented programs in the humanities can be undertaken only by those organizations with large budgets, unrestricted charters, and a staff of specialists. Understanding, like charity, begins at home. Without spending a cent or a centime abroad, it is possible to work internationally if a foundation undertakes to increase public knowledge of international issues and is willing to fund university programs, lecture series, translations, and the like—the ways of helping are almost endless. A foundation whose charter permits it to work abroad, of course, has some advantages; but even where there are legal restrictions, to say nothing of political or financial ones, which keep funding from crossing international boundaries, these factors need not keep imaginations imprisoned.

NOTES

1. Raymond B. Fosdick, *The Story of the Rockefeller Foundation, 1913–1950* (New York: Harper and Bros., 1952), pp. 237–52.

2. This friendship had a fitting memorial in Fosdick's biography, *John D. Rockefeller, Jr.: A Portrait* (New York: Harper & Bros., 1956). Though they were friends for over forty-five years, Fosdick always addressed him as "Mr. Rockefeller."

3. For a brief account of the gifts to the League, see ibid., pp. 388–98, and the collection of Fosdick's correspondence published as *Letters on the League of Nations* (Princeton, N.J.: Princeton University Press, 1966).

4. Quoted in Carlton J. H. Hayes, *France: A Nation of Patriots* (New York: Columbia University Press, 1930), pp. 36, 21.

5. Alexandra Oleson and John Voss, eds., *The Organization of Knowledge in Modern America, 1860–1920* (Baltimore: Johns Hopkins University Press, 1979).

6. Raymond Fosdick, *The Old Savage in the New Civilization* (New York: Doubleday, 1929), p. 25.

7. Ibid., p. 28. For the revealing letter ("Those dreadful memories of dead men hanging on barbed wire won't let me sleep") see Fosdick, *Letters on the League*, p. 100.

8. Dean Rusk, "Notes on Rockefeller Foundation Program," December 1, 1953, an unpublished memo, "Program and Policy," Rockefeller Foundation MSS, Rockefeller Archive Center, New York, N.Y.

9. David Stevens, "The Humanities Program of the Rockefeller Foundation: A Review of the Period 1942–1947," Rockefeller Foundation MSS, p. 5.

10. Burton Fahs, unpublished memo, June 10, 1949, Rockefeller Foundation MSS.

11. Quoted in Burton Fahs to Joel Colton, December 2, 1979, Rockefeller Foundation Files, New York, N.Y.

12. Rockefeller Foundation, *Annual Report*, 1962, p. 35.

13. Peter H. Wood, "What Price Humanism?" undated memo, Rockefeller Foundation MSS.

14. Rockefeller Foundation, *Annual Report*, 1961, p. 14.

15. Ibid., 1968, p. 91.

16. Commission on the Humanities, *The Humanities in American Life* (Berkeley: University of California Press, 1980), p. 25.

17. President's Commission on Foreign Language and International Studies, *Strength through Wisdom: A Report to the President from the President's Commission on Foreign Language and International Studies* (Washington, D.C.: Government Printing Office, 1979), pp. 7–8.

18. Abraham Flexner, *Funds and Foundations: Their Policies, Past and Present* (New York: Harper and Bros., 1952), p. 130.

19. Jacques Barzun, *The House of Intellect* (New York: Harper and Bros., 1959), pp. 182, 189–90.

20. Ibid., p. 191.

21. John Higham, *Writing American History: Essays on Modern Scholarship* (Bloomington: Indiana University Press, 1970), p. 10.

22. Ibid., pp. 10, 24. Higham concludes, "To sum up: the humanities as we know them today in America comprise no meaningful or coherent entity."

23. Charles Burton Fahs, "Widening Our Cultural Horizons," memo, November 30, 1954, appendix to the minutes of the Board of Trustees meeting for November 30–December 1, 1954, Rockefeller Foundation MSS.

24. Quoted in David H. Stevens, *A Time of Humanities: An Oral History: Recollections of David H. Stevens,* ed. Robert Yahnke (Madison: Wisconsin Academy of Sciences, Arts and Letters, 1976), p. 117.

3 / Humanism and the Humanities: An Effort at Definition

W. McNEIL LOWRY

For nearly two decades W. McNeil Lowry presided over the nation's largest and most significant program of private cultural support. In this highly personal essay, Lowry discusses his perceptions of the place of the humanities in modern life, as well as some of the considerations which shaped his own decision making during his tenure at the Ford Foundation.

How difficult it is, in an era when familiar words seem somehow outsized, for those who offer themselves as humanists or seek to define, even to reassert, the place of humanism near the close of another century. Let us put the question to the most cultivated person we can find, and get beyond the embarrassment over large words felt by both the questioner and the questioned. Wystan Auden spoke of "the *ennui* of the cultivated mind," and that will help me to suggest the climate of a discourse I am crudely but purposefully inventing.[1]

The first response is that one must abandon humanism as a way for society, even the most educated or egalitarian, particularly since society has long abandoned the notion, if it ever indeed on any practical or dynamic scale harbored it. We are asked to give up "the great Jeffersonian hope . . . [with] its crystalline power and dignity"—George Steiner's words—"[that] as we learn more, as our imagination becomes more educated, certain kinds of bestiality won't be possible to us any more."[2] And Matthew Arnold is made to appear positively sentimental in believing "that the school, the library, are the great instruments of making man compassionate and humane, and giving to him the realization that any other human being is an infinitely complicated and valuable presence."

A second response is that humanism as a *via media* and the humanist as a practitioner retain only the value, are *reduced* to the value, of historicity. This reaction is not meant as wholly destructive, or even as repudiation. What makes a living community is a shared remembrance of its language and culture. And however tentative we are in moralizing about the best things thought and said in the world, we have seen too clearly what becomes of those who are cut off from any past. Have we had our fill of music without melody, painting without portraiture, architecture without adornment? I do not know, except that the question is precisely the aesthetic and critical crux of the day. But most thoughtful persons can nevertheless imagine a society that has rooted out human memory and have no difficulty in recoiling from it.

A third response—that humanists, if they be both capable and fortunate, are left to cultivate their own gardens—therefore still transcends any obsession with privatism, with "doing one's own thing" in the company of a few friends at most. The humanist is not Socrates' idiot. In one way or another the humanist teaches. The single-mindedness of a capable humanist leads to form, discipline, or technique, and, again, with a little fortune becomes visible to others, if they choose to look. They can take it or leave it, but it is there. There is risk in consciously cultivating one's garden, and it has increased since Voltaire's day. When Auden exiled himself to America, he wrote: "[The] greater the equality of opportunity in a society becomes, the more obvious becomes the inequality of the talent and character among individuals, and the more bitter and personal it must be to fail, particularly for those who have some talent but not enough to win them second or third place."[3]

A fourth response to the humanist's place in society is invariably to contrast it with that of the scientist. Humanists perhaps more than all others have helped to wear out this subject. Auden said (I hope I do not weary you of *him*) that when he found himself in the company of scientists, he felt like a shabby curate who had strayed by mistake into a drawing room full of dukes. Robert Oppenheimer made the familiar observation that no Bacon could any longer have his *Novum Organum,* but honed it by adding that when Einstein came to die there would no longer be one mind that could embrace both modern mathematics and modern physics. He pictured humanists and scientists on either side of a volleyball net exchanging paper airplanes with the word *love* written upon them.

Steiner, like Auden, envies a little the happiness of the young scientist, who says to himself he can do things Newton or even

Einstein could not. "He is moving with the arrow of time . . . for him, the past really is the past. He bears it affection, he bears it respect, it is no way in his way." But the scholar-humanist "walks, as does one troupe of the accursed in Dante's *Inferno,* with his head twisted backward." And Steiner can imagine something even more destructive to any optimism in the humanist: "There is the haunting possibility that we come after the great moments in art and literature, that we come in every sense a long way after, that we are the epilogue to Western genius."[4]

Something akin to this feeling was voiced in the seventeenth century by many writers, philosophers, and moralists. They were living in the old age of the world; not only men but trees and other objects in nature were smaller. Nature itself appeared in throes, and plagues were not the only catastrophic intrusions. But some of the causative factors in this malaise now appear to have been time-bound. The veneration of the ancients had lasted long, and though it continued for more than another century it had in the mid-seventeenth the character of a cliché. Wars were still being fought over points of sheer dogma, and order, if not any longer automatically resting in the divine right of the monarch, was not yet clearly based elsewhere. The individual's responsibility for development of self had been accepted by an elect fraternity, but legal guarantees to that freedom were not part of any social contract. That humanism was also a civic ideal was as old as classic antiquity and stimulated by the Renaissance, but republicanism as a protector of the rights of citizens was tested only sporadically until the end of another century, when the belief that educated citizens would participate in decisions for the common good was given expression as an ideal.

A fifth and most final response to the place of humanism in our world is that if art, philosophy, literature, language are humanizing and civilizing, the political crimes of the twentieth century have to be left as inexplicable. Or if they are *not* to be—but how can we face that question? What if Yeats were a hundredfold right in declaring:

The ceremony of innocence is drowned;
The best lack all conviction, while the worst
Are full of passionate intensity?[5]

Jacobo Timerman, after the experiences recreated in *Prisoner without a Name, Cell without a Number,* concluded: "The chief obsession of the totalitarian mind lies in its need for the world to be clearcut and orderly. Any subtlety, contradiction, or complexity upsets and confuses this notion and becomes intolerable. Whereupon an attempt is made to overcome the intolerable by way of the only method at hand—violence."[6] This appears to me the most illuminating contemporaneous insight into Yeats's "blood-dimmed tide."

Plutarch wrote:

They are wrong who think that politics is like an ocean voyage, or a military campaign, something to be done with a particular end in view, something which leaves off as soon as that end is reached. It is not a public chore, to be got over with. It is a way of life. . . . It is not simply office-holding, it is not just keeping your place, not just raising your voice from the floor, not just ranting on the rostrum with speeches and motions. . . . Politics and philosophy are alike. . . . All your life, all your time, in everything you do, whatever you are doing, is the time for philosophy. And so also it is of politics.[7]

Could it be true, as George Steiner has wondered, that in the humanist ideal, in culture, in morality, there is blackmail, and that in our times "there may have been a kind of enormous spasmodic, animal turning on that ideal"?[8] Then if we hold to the ideal only in silence, are we a part of, or an accomplice to, what Timerman calls "the great silence which appears in every civilized country that passively accepts the inevitability of violence"?[9]

Auden wrote of Kipling:

Others have been concerned with the corruptions of the big city, the ennui of the cultured mind; some sought a remedy in a return to Nature, to childhood, to classical antiquity; others looked forward to a brighter future of liberty, equality and fraternity: they called on the powers of the subconscious, or prayed for the grace of God to inrupt and save their souls; they called on the oppressed to arise and save the world. In Kipling there is none of this, no nostalgia for a Golden Age, no belief in Progress. For him civilization (and consciousness) is a little citadel of light surrounded by a great darkness full of malignant forces and only maintained through the centuries by everlasting vigilance, will-power and self-sacrifice.[10]

It is only the last sentence in that passage which serves my context—the little citadel of light is far away in tone from the garden one cultivates in revulsion at what goes on in the marketplace.

Of the statements of determinism I have encountered none appears more sweeping than Albert Einstein's written in 1929: "Everything is determined, the beginning as well as the end, by forces over which we have no control. It is determined for the insect as well as for the star. Human beings, vegetables, or cosmic dust, we all dance to a mysterious tune, intoned in the distance by an invisible piper."

I do not know the truth of this declaration. But to understand it, even intellectually, to *accept* it, and nevertheless to act as if it is not true, or even to fight against it, is perhaps the highest wisdom. I believe that is also the only response to the beast loosed in our time in a highly cultured and civilized society. If we think only collectively, we do not really penetrate the darkness; we leave nothing between individual human beings and the maximum satisfaction of their physical and material needs. It is when we think of individuals that we dare again to bet on humanity, on humanism, on the humanizing and civilizing forces in art, philosophy, music, literature, and language. However unprovable, even untenable, the wager may be, it has the virtue of necessity. We need it to go on. Without it there are only solipsism, nihilism, and despair.

In thus introducing my remarks, I have perhaps laid myself open to many charges—that I may have violated my assignment; have traduced my own view that the humanities pursue matters of value without defining value as social utility; have contradicted my own style of philanthropy in the humanities, which was content to assume that the acquisition, preservation, and dissemination of knowledge were worthwhile ends in their own right; and have appeared both parochial and chauvinistic by drawing only from Western culture and largely from the English language. Who could now project Rudyard Kipling as a beacon of humanist vigilance, even through Wystan Auden as intermediary?

When I hasten to preempt these charges myself you will rightly understand that my offenses have been purposeful. Obviously there are other options. In *The Humanities in American Life,* the report of a Commission on the Humanities supported by the Rockefeller Foundation, the word *humanism* does not appear. There are, of course, constant references to *humanists* and to *the humanities,* and with eloquence. Examples are plentiful: "The interests and aspirations of many people turn naturally toward the humanities through concern for freedom, moral values, beauty, and knowledge of the past." "Through the humanities we reflect on the fundamental question: What does it mean to be human?" The humanities "reveal how people have tried to make moral, spiritual, and intellectual sense of a world in which irrationality, despair, loneliness, and death are as conspicuous as birth, friendship, hope, and reason."[11]

This commission accepted the disciplinary descriptions of the humanities that have accreted in our own country over the past twenty years, but emphasized that "fields alone do not define the humanities. . . . The essence of the humanities is a spirit or attitude toward humanity." The commission repudiated a "common culture . . . limited to the Western tradition. . . . American society, among the world's most diverse in its cultural origins, should cherish that diversity as a source of constantly renewed strength." But the commission also warned that "there is danger in diversity when it is carried to extremes. No society can flourish if its citizens deny the possibility of a common culture that unites all despite differences in origin, education, and outlook."[12]

So "humanism" can be left . . . where? At any rate, it cannot be left squarely in the middle of one's road, not as the Everest that may prove impassable. This has certainly been the position of humanism in the half century of my own education. Some years ago, so far as I was aware, "humanism" was being invoked from two disparate quarters. The first was the "new humanism" of Paul Elmer More and Irving Babbitt. The second was the mix in French philosophy and literary journalism produced by Jacques Maritain and Julien Benda. The new humanism appeared academic, thin, and attenuated. Maritain produced almost the same response, and the relativism of Benda, the indiscriminate selections from experience, slid easily into solipsism or existentialism. Far more disciplined appeared Santayana's skepticism and animal faith. He may have sniffed at "humanism," but his naturalism was kin to Montaigne's.

So at this juncture even in our own short span, we can accept "the essence of the humanities [as] a spirit or attitude toward humanity," rather than strive and fail to erect a philosophical system out of humanism. No doubt we realize the price we pay for abandoning the word, nevertheless. We know that ignorant, misguided, or vicious men in the United States are making even now a systematic attack on humanism through having equated it with atheism and everything evil. Their real enemies are toleration, free inquiry, and individual liberty, and however gross, there is Manichean insight in their perversity. We cannot enter the lists on their own terms, so we erect defenses against censorship, coercion, repression, and the tyranny of the majority.

Note that except in spirit or attitude the humanities are not directly enjoined in this comedy—unless analysis of the situation of the humanities is intrinsically an inventory of the shortcomings in an educational system! But it is not only humanists who teach people to read and write. And the ability to read and write does not prevent all people from equating humanism with atheism, or from any other devil theory.

In the United States, humanists, educators, and those who promote government activities in the field generally agree about a broad cluster of disciplines embraced by the humanities, and I wonder if we can perhaps stipulate their terminology for reference. They include language; literature; philosophy; history; religion; cultural anthropology; the history of science and law; the history, theory, and criticism of the arts; and the humanistic aspects of the social sciences. Sometimes they lay claim to the creative and performing arts beyond their historical and theoretical analysis, stressing the experience of art and literature as a preeminent medium toward moral, spiritual, and intellectual sense in the world.

When we begin to ask ourselves what we can do, or whether we should do anything at all about international cooperation in philanthropy in these fields, the starting point is crucial, even desperate, demanding a rigor and an honesty which offend our senses.

We have all, I think, had experience of intercultural programs on one scale or another, and we know how hard it is to concentrate on cultures and their meaning to people amid the inevitable glare of politics, global abstractions, economic forces, political camps. It is frustrating and ridiculous, but I am afraid nevertheless true, that these doctrinal winds blow even upon a simple program exchanging persons. What is "the West"? A common cultural tradition? An economic system? An armed camp? Which? What is "the Third World"? A global scattering of countries united by poverty and hatred of a colonial past? As powerful cultural influences as those two evils constitute, do they forge a common culture despite even more ancient and disparate roots and influences? Suppose that what we call Third World nations were all at once independent and economically stable; how many cultures would they represent, and what then would be a common motive for collaboration? What is "the Second World," and what makes it one?

I know how stupid these questions can sound by now; they are an irritant, but perhaps a necessary one. For one thing, they remind us forcibly of the great debt we owe to the patience of the individual scholars who seek to ignore the large surface, the glare of politics and xenophobia, and uncover for us the real, the trustworthy, underneath. In their studies or on location they *pursue* knowledge before abstracting it even as "culture." And only for myself I can now answer two questions I left dangling: The person who can best succeed in penetrating other cultures has first mastered his own, and the starting point for cooperation in philanthropy is in the criteria of humanistic scholarship, or rather our willingness to prosecute its standards, to make choices even at the risk of goring both our own oxen and those of our neighbors. Scholar-humanists may indeed be left to cultivate their own gardens if they choose. We need to know what other cultures *are* before we know their differences from our own. But philanthropy in the humanities is also a profession and an exercise of choice, and can assay the same hard concentration beneath the glare of political and global forces.

A little-publicized experience of my own made some kind of test of that generalization. In 1968 I was able to seize an opportunity to support artists and humanists in Greece through a unique extension of the Ford Foundation program I directed in the United States. It was made timely because of the need and oppression of artists and scholars created by the colonels who had seized power in that country. In the hundreds of choices of individuals and groups over a period of six years I asked the advice only of Greek artists and scholars, not American, and of neither the United States nor the Greek governments. The only criteria were those of talent and quality, a humanist ideal no matter how commonplace in philanthropy in these fields.

But steadily and publicly pursuing only those criteria, without regard to huge political forces within Greece or between the United States and Greece—even the official U.S. toleration or support of the colonels—had some remarkable effects. Through six years and the expenditures of our $6 million, Papadopoulos and Patakos successively backed away from outlawing the program. And freedom of individual expression was almost every day illustrated, though never promulgated as a concept. What was supported was the opportunity of scholars and artists to do the work of their own choice. If by their own political activities they were imprisoned, and a few were, it was not because they accepted our grants, and we found ways to complete the payments contracted for.

But suppose the Ford Foundation *had* offered a political concept, the freedom of expression, as rationale for the program? This is not a question I am asking in retrospect, but one I lived with from the first moment in the most tortuous ways, though not at all so painfully as did my associates and grantees in Greece. Among all the consequences flowing from such a rationale, perhaps three were paramount.

First, we could have lost both our strict standards of selectivity and even our freedom to work at all in areas so sensitive to a dictatorship. You will not be surprised that among the applicants were many friends of the government and even one or two branches of its bureaucracy.

Second, we would have had little justification for rejecting applications from Greek exiles in other countries, and had we not rejected them, not the foundation but all its grantees in Greece would have paid a terrible price. There is a legitimate foundation objective in aiding defectors from dictatorship, but it must be separated absolutely from a program to keep free creation and scholarship alive in a given country. As George Seferis wrote in the first year after the colonels' coup, "So long as there is not freedom to speak in my own land, there is not for me free speech anywhere."[13]

Third, how could the foundation have defended such a rationale for concentrating support of artists and humanists in only one dictatorship among many?

Lest you think my putting these questions either academic or self-serving, I can assure you that only by the assumption of values underlying the humanities were the results of the program achieved. Inevitably, the foundation was attacked for *not* having the principle my beleaguered Greek deputy and I were acting upon. The very fact that our selections succeeded in justifying only artistic talent or scholarly ability meant that the Ford Foundation *must* have had another motive for offering the program!

Could it be that the foundation wished to "alienate" artists and scholars in Greece, assuaging their discontent and therefore their opposition to the colonels? It was difficult not only for the press but even for some applicants in the program to see only the humanistic principle on which it worked. In Greece, moreover, there is not much experience with any philanthropic tradition. Over and over I was asked what the individual was expected to do in return for the foundation. To concentrate only on his or her own creative work was an answer difficult to accept. The "blackmail" George Steiner describes can be felt even in a free and selfless act. In Greece it was not only Communists but many democrats who feared to prove themselves naive. They accepted the results of the program they could not avoid seeing. They respected the artists and scholars consulted in reaching them. But they nevertheless attacked the unknown "real" objective underneath, and even more maddening, they often tried to include me among the naive, the innocent, the duped. Perhaps I was a humanist token in the Ford Foundation to conceal its "real" objectives. Or even, perhaps, I was subverting my own institution.

I have earlier noted Jacobo Timerman's conclusion that "any subtlety, contradiction, or complexity upsets and confuses" the totalitarian mind "in its need for the world to be clearcut and orderly." We see symptoms of this confusion everywhere, even in nations that are not dictatorships and have not, in Timerman's words, attempted "to overcome the intolerable" by violence.[14]

If I have dwelt overlong on an international program in the humanities simple and direct in its object, it was to make the point that in this time nothing is any longer simple, certainly no system of values. What one person or one group of people acts upon as motive spring is swept into a sea of relativism with everything else. The task for the humanities, in short, is much more difficult than in the past, than even at the outset of our own century. Whether humanists express them or not, the intellectual and moral values underlying the humanities are disturbing to many forces in the society and plainly hostile to others. Far from being taken for granted, if indeed they ever could be, they are at the least confusing and easily subject to misprision. If the goal of international cooperation in the humanities were left at universal literacy, perhaps it would not prove intolerable, even if impractical. Anything more, even historicity, can awake the tribunals and their right of reply.

Then could it be true that in the support of the humanities we gain very little by leaving their values unexpressed? Perhaps we avoid some embarrassment, but is it any longer the embarrassment of stating the obvious? Scholars, educators, philanthropists concerned with the humanities constantly remind themselves and others that a liberal education for many persons no longer produces a common set of values, even a common body of knowledge. In the United States a greater proportion of young people than ever is in college, but even periodicals aimed at the broad public can describe the new core curriculum at Harvard as having no core and affording less general education for the majority of students than the curriculum it supplanted. I think it may be that the sober tone of the report of the Rockefeller Commission on the Humanities emanated chiefly from testing similar conclusions at all levels of the U.S. educational system. (The commission nevertheless took pains to point out curricula or schools in which the outlook is positive.)

Heightened consciousness of the values underlying the humanities is forced upon humanists by the greater difficulty of their task, by generational losses in memory, and by the welter of stereotypes more and more abstract and global through the speeding up not only of information but of propaganda. But it is also forced as a matrix of their morale. All men and women, perhaps, today find less hope in thinking collectively. It is, as Steiner said, when we think of individuals that we dare to wager on humanity. The "little citadels of light" have to mean more than gardens of self-indulgence, however neatly cultivated. The humanities near the end of our century may be not an important but an indispensable means of civilizing the world. That is a very large statement, but the very odds, the difficulties in the way, make it more probable. The essence of the humanities is the ability to make choices.

We begin, therefore, with the individual: the individual scholar, within whatever culture, which means the scholar's work, the opportunity to pursue it, preserve it, disseminate it, exchange it with peers; the individual not yet a scholar, this person's training and chance for personal confrontation with living mentors of scholarship and art. The picture of one culture, even of one country, in the press of another is important but never adequate and often distorted. History, literature, philosophy deepen and widen the base, but one gifted artist or writer can sometimes make it indelible. So along with the individual as scholar, as teacher, as student, we begin with the individual as artist.

If these remarks seem to translate into familiar operations of philanthropy, rather than into policy, I submit to that charge. I have tried to say that the impossibility of proving that the school and the library have been the great instruments by which to civilize man is itself a reason for heightened concentration on the humanities. And believing that the work of the scholar-humanist and the artist, in free choice, is what we must begin with, I distrust and, for myself at least, disavow our ability to cooperate on a common policy for the Third World, the West, or the Communist world. Somehow we have to concentrate on cultures and their meaning to people despite the steady glaring of politics, global abstractions, economic forces, and armed camps.

There are many persons today who go farther than George Steiner in wondering whether "we come after the great moments in art and literature, . . . we come in every sense a long way after."[15] They fear that our cultural history has moved into the realm of eschatology. And sometimes they fear that the cultivation of their own gardens is about to be ended through nuclear radiation.

If any of us agreed, would it make any difference in our concentration on the humanizing and civilizing forces in art, philosophy, music, literature, and language? I wonder. Would we nevertheless not be led to make a choice that has the virtue of necessity? Was it not the choice of ancients known in many, many cultures in the long past of the world?

NOTES

1. W. H. Auden, *Forewords and Afterwords* (New York: Random House, 1973), p. 352.
2. "George Steiner on Literature, Language, and Culture," transcript of "Bill Moyers' Journal," May 22, 1981, Journal Graphics, New York.
3. W. H. Auden, *The Dyer's Hand and Other Essays* (New York: Random House, 1968), p. 245.
4. "Steiner on Literature, Language, and Culture."
5. William Butler Yeats, "The Second Coming," in *The Collected Poems of W. B. Yeats* (New York: Macmillan Co., 1956), p. 185.
6. Jacobo Timerman, *Prisoner without a Name, Cell without a Number* (New York: Alfred A. Knopf, 1981), p. 95.
7. Plutarch, *Moralia,* trans. Frank Cole Babbitt (New York: G. P. Putnam's Sons, 1976), 15:10.
8. "Steiner on Literature, Language, and Culture."

9. Timerman, *Prisoner without a Name*, p. 51.
10. Auden, *Forewords and Afterwords*.
11. Commission on the Humanities, *The Humanities in American Life* (Berkeley: University of California Press, 1980), p. 1.
12. Ibid., pp. 2–3.
13. George Seferis to the dean of the Harvard University Graduate School.
14. Timerman, *Prisoner without a Name*, p. 95.
15. "Steiner on Literature, Language, and Culture."

4 / Business Support of the Humanities: A Global Perspective

DANELLA SCHIFFER

This essay shifts the focus from the private foundations to the corporate arena. As Danella Schiffer explains, corporate giving outpaced private foundation gifts for the first time in 1979 and has continued to grow since that time. How does the philosophy of the corporate donor differ from that of a private foundation such as Rockefeller or Ford? Although a few private foundations have significantly underwritten the humanities, corporations have failed to follow their lead. Schiffer explains why businesses have been slow to fund the humanities and outlines a few harbingers of growing interest in these fields.

Few would deny that the humanities in the United States are in deep trouble. Student enrollments in humanistic studies are down, with over half of American college students enrolled in professional and vocational programs. Support, too, is down, with the likelihood of further erosions. A fundamental reason may be that the humanities are perceived as lacking relevance to modern life, and humanists are viewed as ivory-tower scholars isolated from everyday realities. Clearly, this has been the prevailing viewpoint of the business sector, and its support of the humanities bears testimony to this claim. The present essay examines that viewpoint, along with some positive trends, and raises critical questions which need to be addressed if business support of the humanities is to be increased worldwide.

AN OVERVIEW OF CORPORATE PHILANTHROPY

For the first time in U.S. history, total corporate philanthropic dollars during 1979 exceeded those of private foundations. With giving from all sources amounting to $43.46 billion, corporations accounted for $2.45 billion, or 5.6 percent. Private foundations accounted for $2.24 billion, or 5.3 percent. However, while actual corporate philanthropic dollars increased from 1978 to 1979, the ratio of contributions to pretax net income dropped from 1.09 percent during 1978 to 1.04 percent during 1979. In addition, only 25–30 percent of the approximately two million corporations in the United States report making any charitable contributions, and only about 6 percent contribute more than $500 annually. One can conclude that corporate philanthropy, while already impressive, has not nearly reached its potential.

The accompanying tabulation is a breakdown of the categories in which corporate philanthropic dollars were spent during 1979 (based on Conference Board data):[1]

1979 total = $2.45 billion

Health and welfare (including United Ways)	35.0%
Education (all education, including higher education)	37.7%
Culture and art	9.9%
Civic and other	11.6%

It is worth noting that this was the first year in which corporate giving to education surpassed that to health and welfare. Higher education was the prime beneficiary and received an all-time high of $870 million—a 17.6 percent increase over 1978 and more than double the 1975 amount.

Statistics alone, however, say very little about the nature of corporate philanthropy. Clearly, it would be impractical to include here a detailed accounting. Yet at the risk of oversimplification, one can highlight some key characteristics which distinguish corporate giving from that of other donors.

First and foremost, corporate philanthropy, unlike private foundation and individual philanthropy, is not a form of benevolent charity. Corporations are accountable to a number of publics for their philanthropic activities—namely, shareholders, employees, and consumers. Therefore, corporate philanthropy is characteristically driven by corporate self-interest. Irving Kristol, in a March 21, 1977, *Wall Street Journal* article, stated the case very aptly: "Charity involves dispensing your own money, not your stockholders'. When you give away your own money, you can be as foolish, as whimsical as you like. But when you give away your stockholders' money, your philanthropy must serve longer-term interests of the corporation. Corporate philanthropy should not be, cannot be disinterested."

The ways in which corporate self-interest is manifested can be illustrated by the distribution of corporate support to colleges and universities. The usual pattern is that corporations favor those institutions which directly benefit their business. For example, a given corporation will perceive it to be in its own interest to support institutions with academic specialties relevant to the particular industry (e.g., engineering, finance, actuarial science). Presumably, this support will help ensure a steady flow of managerial and professional talent to meet recruitment needs. Also favored are those schools which provide such benefits as relevant research activities, library services, and perhaps even educational opportunities for employees and their families.

A second, related pattern is that corporations tend to favor those issues and causes which are related to their business. For example, Weyerhaeuser Company is interested in the field of forest management, while Mattel is more concerned with the needs of children.

A third important characteristic concerns the geographic focus of corporate grant making. Generally, corporations concentrate their philanthropic dollars in those communities with a company presence (i.e., plants and offices). Thus, corporate philanthropic interests are characteristically more local than national in scope.

Next, corporations tend to avoid supporting controversial causes, in order to avoid unnecessary conflicts with those constituencies to which they are accountable.

Finally, compared with private foundations, corporations tend to give smaller amounts to more organizations. To illustrate this point, of the fifteen largest foundations by *number* of grants awarded (as opposed to size of assets or size of individual grants), eleven are corporate foundations. Interestingly, most of them have total annual budgets of less than one-third that of the Carnegie Corporation, which is usually listed among the fifteen largest foundations, measured in assets. The purpose of spreading money around more thinly is to enable a corporation to appeal to a broader constituency.

Clearly, corporations expect to get something in return for their philanthropic activities. Direct and indirect benefits, including goodwill, are important factors in their decision making on contributions.

BUSINESS AND THE HUMANITIES

Support   Let us now turn to a look at corporate support of the humanities. First, it should be noted that there is little unanimity among corporate executives on exactly what constitutes the humanities. According to the National Endowment for the Humanities, the humanities incorporate "history, philosophy, languages, literature, linguistics, archaeology, jurisprudence, history and criticism of the arts, ethics, comparative religion, and those aspects of the social sciences employing historical or philosophical approaches. This last category includes cultural anthropology, sociology, political theory, international relations and other subjects concerned with questions of value and not with quantitative matters."[2] Given the sweeping and imprecise nature of this definition, it is no wonder that businesspeople are unclear about the exact meaning of the term.

With rare exceptions, humanities categories do not appear in reports of corporate giving. Typically, the humanities are lumped under Arts and Culture, and even then, what may be perceived by corporate executives as a humanities grant may not really be one. And to confuse matters even further, humanities grants may even be listed under the Education category. Given this problem in reporting, it is virtually impossible to determine the extent to which corporations actually support humanistic undertakings. A good guess might be that less than 5 percent of 1979's $2.45 billion in corporate philanthropy was so earmarked. It has been suggested that corporations place a low priority on giving to the humanities because this area is seen as having little relevance to a corporation's well-being. Robert Mercer, president of Goodyear Tire and Rubber Company, stated the general sentiments of the private sector in a recent National Chamber Foundation publication, *Corporate Philanthropy in the Eighties:* Corporate support of higher education "should be in those areas of higher education that will produce informed people, who, as graduates of the system, will enter business with the right principles and understanding of our business society. . . . And that kind of training cannot be established from a chair in Medieval English."[3]

In a similar, but more positive, vein, Exxon Corporation states in its 1980 contributions report: "Another question we have been exploring is how a foundation like this one can help the humanities and social sciences, especially in their relationship to business, government and other social institutions. How can we facilitate the flow of insights from history and literature and sociology and philosophy and religion into the mainstream of American life?" Exxon's message is that the humanities should be important to the business sector insofar as they have relevance to American life, of which business is an integral part.

Liberal Arts Graduates as Business Employees   Over the past decade, education has become highly specialized to meet the technical demands of modern life. Is there still a place for the liberal arts curriculum, then, amid such market-driven specialties as medicine, law, finance, and computer programming, to name only a few? What can the liberal arts graduate do to earn a living in this era of the "Third Wave"?[4] Clearly, academia has become a very limited option.

During recent years, there has been a growing respect among business leaders for the talents of those with a grounding in the humanities. In a pamphlet produced by the Council for Financial Aid to Education, Roger Smith, chairman of General Motors Corporation, explains persuasively why business needs the liberal arts. As an industrial company, GM recruits many more engineers, scientists, technicians, and graduates of business schools than writers, historians, linguists, or social scientists. However, Smith readily admits that "the world in which today's business leader must make decisions is far too eclectic for the overspecialized specialist."[5] He then builds a case for preparing a new kind of specialist, one who has combined the liberal arts with a technical specialty.

The American Telephone and Telegraph Company (AT&T) has gone a step further by welcoming liberal arts graduates without technical specialties. As the United States' largest employer, AT&T hires about six thousand college graduates annually, of which approximately one-third are liberal arts graduates with majors in the humanities, social science, math, and science. The remaining two-thirds have degrees in engineering and business. In a twenty-year longitudinal study of AT&T managers that compared those with a liberal arts background to those in engineering and business, the liberal arts majors, notably those with humanities and social science backgrounds, initially showed the greatest potential for middle management. Furthermore, over the twenty-year period they did in fact advance further than those with other majors.

Steps to promote the employability of liberal arts graduates have been taken by educational institutions. For example, in 1978 the Graduate School of Business Administration at New York University, in cooperation with the New York State Office of Education and the National Endowment for the Humanities, launched a Careers in Business program: a six-week session of intensive business courses for select students with Ph.D.'s in the humanities and social sciences. At the end of the session, students are interviewed by corporate recruiters for possible employment. By all accounts, the program has been highly successful, and it continues to function with the assistance of corporate support— about $40,000 annually from ten companies.

Humanists as Consultants   Business has come to recognize the value of humanists not only as full-time employees but also as consultants with the expertise needed to help it function in an increasingly complex world. More and more, humanists are being called upon to assist management sort out a variety of ethical issues which could have far-reaching consequences for a company's short- and long-term viability. Issues concerning product safety, environmental impact, and corporate presence in foreign cultures are but a few which lend themselves to humanistic clarifications.

SOME THOUGHTS ON BUSINESS SUPPORT OF THE HUMANITIES WORLDWIDE

A discussion of corporate interest in the humanities on a world-wide basis is an exceedingly difficult task for a number of reasons: First, there is a dearth of written information on international corporate philanthropic activities generally, let alone particular reference to the humanities. It is also exceedingly difficult to communicate with corporate executives abroad. Another major problem is that the lack of consensus among corporate executives on a definition of the humanities is most apparent on an international scale. It may be useful, however, again using the U.S. experience as an example, to review international corporate philanthropic practices briefly and to lay out some of the more central issues which need to be addressed if ever an attempt is made to increase support worldwide.

There are essentially two ways to define international corporate philanthropy. On the one hand it can refer to domestic corporate philanthropy worldwide, that is, to corporate philanthropic activities throughout the world of companies in their own countries. Or it can refer to the philanthropic activities of multinational corporations in host countries. If we accept the latter definition, then we need to know something about how corporations make grants in host countries.

In the United States, the administrative practices of international corporate philanthropy vary considerably among corporations. Typically, responsibilities are decentralized among the corporate offices abroad, with local managers having major say for the philanthropic activities within their geographical areas. This arrangement, in fact, leads to the one common ground rule: No grant is made to an organization providing services abroad without the approval of the local corporate office.

The major differences in corporate practices concern the role of corporate headquarters, the decision-making process, and who bears the cost.

Role of Corporate Headquarters   At corporate headquarters, responsibility for international philanthropy can rest in any one of several areas: the contributions department or foundation, the public affairs department, or the international division. The role of the headquarters may be to collect and maintain information on the philanthropic activities of the overseas offices, to provide direction or consultation to the overseas managers with philanthropic responsibility, and/or to recommend grants to U.S. tax-exempt organizations providing services in other countries (with approval of the local management).

Decision-Making Process   The decision-making process varies not only among corporations but also within corporations, depending on circumstances surrounding grant requests. In some cases, a local office has complete authority over grants. In other cases, a local office may make grant recommendations to headquarters, where approval is granted or denied. Another possibility is that headquarters may introduce a prospective grantee to the local office (especially if the prospective grantee has U.S. tax-exempt status), and then make a decision on the basis of input from the local office.

Who Bears the Cost? Grants can be paid by the corporate contributions department or foundation at headquarters, by the local offices recommending the grants, or by a combination of both. It should be noted, however, that U.S. corporations are unlikely to make grants unless they are tax deductible, or business-related so that they can be justified as business expenses.

Grants made by U.S. multinational corporations must typically meet two criteria: (1) The grant should provide a benefit to the local office (e.g., build a school to train potential new employees); (2) the grant should serve the company's local employees and their communities. Clearly, as with domestic corporate philanthropy, self-interest is paramount.

A major characteristic of international corporate philanthropy worth mentioning is that of conservatism. There are several reasons for this posture. Grant officers typically feel that they lack adequate knowledge about other cultures and wish to avoid possibly upsetting the status quo with grants that are culture-biased. Furthermore, such grants could be perceived as an attempt of foreign countries to impart foreign values. Conservatism is also driven by the need to avoid antagonizing host governments. So, for example, it may be entirely appropriate for a company operating in South Africa to fund a training program for potential black employees. However, it would be highly risky from a business point of view to support the publication of a literary piece which is critical of apartheid and suggests the overthrow of the South African government. The guiding principle adopted by most U.S. multinational corporations, then, has not been to get deeply involved in the internal affairs of host countries.

Finally, mention should be made of the issue surrounding philanthropy in developed versus less-developed countries. Clearly, the needs of the people in a less-developed country are quite different from those of a developed nation. Support to build a library in a village afflicted by disease and starvation not only would be inappropriate but would smack of insensitivity. This is not to imply that the humanities are irrelevant to the people of less-developed countries. On the contrary, the initiation of a literacy program could be a very legitimate contribution under appropriate circumstances.

Given the complexities surrounding international corporate philanthropy, increasing support of the humanities on a worldwide basis will be a formidable task. For U.S. multinational corporations, some of the more central questions surrounding philanthropy in other countries include:

• How will the grant benefit the company and its employees?
• Will the grant be consistent with the host country's governmental policies?
• Will the grant be appropriate to the culture?
• Will the grant be responsive to the real needs of the people?

Those seeking grants for the humanities must be prepared to answer these questions, at the very least.

SUMMARY

We have seen that in the United States, the amount of corporate support to the humanities is moderated by two primary tendencies: First, corporate philanthropy is driven by corporate self-interest, so that a given company will support those institutions and activities that directly serve it, bring goodwill, or improve the community or communities in which it does business. Second, for the most part, the humanities are perceived as worthy in their own right, but certainly not crucial to the health of the private sector. As a result, corporate philanthropic dollars earmarked for the humanities are relatively insignificant.

Fortunately, however, business leaders are beginning to develop a stronger appreciation for the contributions that humanists can make to business. This turn of events could prove to be an effective lever to pry loose expanded giving to humanistic undertakings. Simply, the implication is that corporate support of the humanities has the potential of increasing dramatically as its relevance to the private sector is made more apparent. But in order for this situation to come about, it may be necessary for humanists to rethink their mission. Also needed will be a better definition of the humanities, one which businesspeople will be able to grasp. Finally, humanists must be willing to market the humanities, promoting their importance to society and business.

NOTES

1. The Conference Board is an independent, not-for-profit research institution specializing in economics and management research for business, government, labor, and other institutions.
2. National Endowment for the Humanities, *Seventeenth Annual Report,* 1982, p. 14.
3. National Chamber Foundation, *Corporate Philanthropy in the Eighties* (Washington, D.C.: National Chamber Foundation, 1980), p. 3.
4. Alvin Toffler, *The Third Wave* (New York: William Morrow and Co., 1980).
5. Roger Smith, *Why Business Needs the Liberal Arts* (New York: Council for Financial Aid to Education, 1981), p. 3.

5 / *Discussions*

FOUNDATIONS, GOVERNMENT, AND THE HUMANITIES

The conference discussions adopted a dual focus, examining both foundation trends and patterns of cultural support. Waldemar A. Nielsen of the Aspen Institute counterpointed Danella Schiffer's corporate overview by drawing attention to the changing role of governmental support in his extensive and highly detailed analysis of the impact of the Reagan administration and its policies on the humanities. He then suggested several options and alternatives available to foundations and their posture vis-à-vis government in the American context, peppering his remarks with a few comparative comments about some of the implications for foundation policy in the 1980s. Because of the breadth and importance of Nielsen's statement, his commentary has been included in its entirety.

Nielsen began his discussion with a few figures explaining "where the flows of funding for the humanities come from in the United States." As he was quick to point out: "Although we have the most detailed data on a very up-to-date basis about the chemical fertilizer business, for example, and about the sales of every kind of manufactured object, we have really nothing that you can take seriously in the way of data with regard to funding in the field of the humanities. The best guesses that I can offer, which are guesses that are more or less shared by people like Robert Lumiansky of the American Council of Learned Societies and others who follow these things in the United States, are about as follows: that at least 90 percent—more likely, something like 95 percent—of the funding for the teaching and the basic scholarly resources in the humanities, that is, libraries, comes from the general support of educational institutions—that is, the general support of secondary education in the United States, the general support of colleges and universities, and the general support of libraries. Only about 5 percent, roughly, comes in the form of direct grants from government and from private sources for the support of projects in the humanities.

"Now, if we try to separate that into categories, how does it split between government and private sources? As all of you are well aware, secondary education in the United States is overwhelmingly a state-funded activity. Parochial schools are not inconsequential, but they are relatively minor in relation to the publicly supported secondary institutions. In the area of higher education, again, the government is heavily predominant, although there is a significant private factor, and certainly in qualitative terms the private element of American higher education is extremely important. If we're talking about the support of libraries, that's even more overwhelmingly a government-funded institutional apparatus.

I will not attempt to try to be even slightly precise about this. For example, I'm not going to try to calculate into this the costs and benefits for the humanities from private book publishing. But it would be my guess that if we split the support of the teaching and research and other activities in the humanities between government and the private side, it certainly would be 80 percent and I would guess more toward 90 percent that comes from government and a relatively small fraction from the private side. And ranking the United States with other advanced democratic societies, that 90 percent from government is on the low side, compared to the situation in France, Germany, Italy, and Japan, for example, where the proportions are probably more between 95 percent and 100 percent. In other words, if we're talking about the financial support and sustenance of the humanities in any sort of conventional definition of the scope of that field, government is overwhelmingly the principal funding source.

"Now, I just want to say a word or two about the Reagan administration and its new policy initiatives with respect to the humanities. We've all been aware that private philanthropy is an institutional arrangement that lives at the sufferance of the state. We're all aware, I'm sure, that there are those states that actively and sometimes totally suppress private philanthropy as a threat on various ideological grounds, a threat represented in the form of independent centers of influence. There are states that more or less tolerate foundations, neither offering significant positive tax incentives for their creation nor imposing severe constraints on their creation or on their freedom of action. Then there are a few countries where the philanthropic tradition is encouraged, and I suppose it would not just be an expression of patriotic prejudice if I said that I thought the United States is probably in that group of countries; that in terms of tax incentives, freedom of action, etcetera, it is a society in which this aspect of pluralism is particularly encouraged.

"Now, there was a time in the 1950s in the United States when, although the tax privileges for the creation and maintenance of foundations continued to be upheld, a political atmosphere of suspicion of foundations resulted in constraints being imposed on them. The Reagan administration presents a rather curious paradox. As part of a general philosophy of trying to restrict and lessen the role of government in the affairs of the society, the Reagan people have repeatedly emphasized their support for the idea of private initiative, not only in the business, profit-making sphere, but in the nonprofit area as well. The president and other leading members of the administration have repeatedly emphasized the very important role that they feel and hope that private sources of funding will play, not only in the human services area but in the general scientific, intellectual, and cultural life of society.

"At the same time, as part of the economic program of the new administration, they have proposed legislation which has now been enacted, which will strike very severely at the entire nonprofit sector, including foundations, of course, but also a vast number of other nonprofit institutions. It has certainly made an observer like me much more aware than I've ever been formerly that it is not just the legal framework of philanthropy that government establishes but that government also, by its tax policies, by its social and human services programs, and by its general economic policies, has an enormous effect on the whole range of such private sector activities.

"Very briefly, the Reagan administration's social program cuts, which are part of this effort to balance the national budget, will strike very heavy blows in education, the arts, state-supported institutions—high schools, colleges, and universities—and private higher education and secondary education. During the last twenty years, our private nonprofit institutions have become increasingly dependent on government funding, to the point where Harvard, for example, depends for about 55 percent of its total income on government, and MIT for more like 75 percent. And many social welfare and other institutions are even more dependent. So that the government's cutbacks in social programs—the reduction of grants and contracts with nonprofit institutions of various kinds, the reduction of student aid programs and research grants—hit these institutions very heavily.

"The tax policies of the new administration were not intended to damage the flow of private giving in the country, but it is the view of a good many prominent economists that the effect of the Reagan tax policy will be to reduce incentives for private philanthropic giving significantly. In effect, reducing the top tax rates in the United States has caused something like a 65 percent increase in what economists call the cost of giving. Until now, a wealthy individual could give $1 to charity and save 70 cents of that dollar because of the taxes that he saved. In other words, it would cost him 30 cents to give a dollar. That top tax rate has now been reduced to 50 percent, so it now costs him 50 cents to give a dollar to charity. On the basis of previous donor behavior, it is expected that this increase in the cost of giving is going to affect giving very significantly. And since it is the wealthy givers who tend to give to humanistic institutions and activities—education and so on (middle- and lower-income donors give to churches, primarily)—these tax effects on humanistic activity in the United States may well be considerable.

"Now, that being so, what are some of the alternative postures that a private philanthropic institution can take vis-à-vis government? The alternatives that American foundations in fact could adopt would include the following. One is simply to ignore government, to say, 'We're a foundation, we have a limited amount of money, we have a charter given us by our donor and we're going to go ahead and support, say, the Department of Romance Languages at Emory University, and we're not going to worry about the whole national climate and complexities of funding.' I would call that the posture of being indifferent to government.

"The second stance is the pilot fish idea, namely, that foundations will attempt to be innovative and creative and experimental. They will try to identify new and promising kinds of things that might be done by government. When these experiments prove their worth, in time they will attract government funding and sustenance, and foundations will thereby perform a creative, innovative role in the society. Obviously this can be a very self-serving attitude, but on the other hand, there are some splendid examples where this approach has indeed produced very significant consequences.

"A third posture (one that very few foundations choose) is to be a monitor and critic of government policies. This is hazardous, even for American foundations, but there are those that sometimes play this role very usefully.

"A fourth alternative is to consider the foundation's role as being supplementary to that of government, a gap-filler—that is, to scan the flows of government funding to see where there may be omissions or gaps that need to be filled, and then to offset or compensate for deficiencies or distortions in government activity.

"A fifth possibility is to be a collaborator and partner of government. This is an idea that has ebbed and flowed at various times in America. It seems to be an increasingly popular idea among American foundations at the present time, as this period of austerity descends upon us. We talk more and more about the possibilities of collaborative and joint activity, not only between private foundations and governments but also between private foundations and corporate foundations, and among private foundations themselves. It's hard to be against cooperation in principle, and it is a theme that you will find in the recent reports of the Ford Foundation.

"And finally on my list of alternative postures is the attempt to be an instrument of government—that is, 'Come use us, call on us for national service. Allow us to participate in the great new adventure.' There are a number of foundations in the United States, and I think from my observations there are a few in Europe, too, that do not object to this kind of call to perform national service. Obviously these are not mutually exclusive categories, and any one foundation may at one time or another do some or all of these kinds of things.

"Given the preponderance of government and given, at least in the American context and probably in Europe and even Japan, too, the prospect of a period of real austerity in the 1980s, how might a foundation try to take these considerations into account? This is a time when, even more than normally, we've got to focus our efforts on some deliberate priorities and concepts of the role of our particular foundations. This is not in any way to suggest that all foundations ought to define their roles in the same terms. In fact, it's the glory of this institution that various foundations are or should be free to define their roles in different ways. But a definition of role consciously arrived at by the institution, as well as a set of relevant programs, is essential for effectiveness.

"And the goals must be realistic. In the case of American foundations, at least, there has often been a grandiosity of objective that simply didn't match the financial or intellectual resources of the institution, more a form of vanity than serious program definition.

"Given these general facts about funding and problems in the field, I feel that foundations even more than in the past must now focus on excellence, on supporting the creative individual, and on selectively filling the vacuum being created, again in the American context at least, by the withdrawal of government support. They must seek not to dissipate their meager resources on sustenance of large institutions but to concentrate on individuals and particular projects of creativity and excellence. Finally, it is most important that the foundations, either directly or through some of their grants, participate vigorously in debates on public policy, including that with respect to the funding of the humanities."

Nielsen's comments generated keen discussion, particularly among the American participants. "At a time when there is a real crisis, you have to ask yourself how you envision the encouragement of the next generation of scholarship," noted Francis X. Sutton of the Ford Foundation. "It's very clear that it is going to have a very bleak economic future, because there is a deterioration in the real income of university staffs, which is the main source of livelihood for humanistic scholars. There will also be the problem of too many candidates for the available positions; many will fall and few will be chosen. It is clear that foundations are not going to be able to meet the basic problems of real income of the scholarly professions in the next generation. What one can do is to facilitate the selection and the encouragement of the best of the new generation, to make sure that excellence will not be lost. That directs one's attention to national mechanisms for the identification, encouragement, and development of talent."

Joel Colton of the Rockefeller Foundation added some reflections about the need for cooperation with government, and among foundations in general, for "in a time of inflation, when foundation funds don't go as far as they once did, it is especially important that foundations work together with other foundations and private sources of support."

"The idea of cooperation in a period of austerity is very much à la mode," commented Nielsen.

"Not only à la mode, but de rigueur," parried Colton.

Sutton then raised the issue of whether the government was shouldering a fair measure of responsibility, or whether foundations had been required to pick up an inequitable portion of the burden in important fields. "Foundations have often done things that ought to be the government's responsibility," he said. "For a good many years the Ford Foundation supplied 75 percent of the research money for Chinese studies. For any part of the world as important as China, that should have been a governmental responsibility. We ought not to have been doing that. And we still have a very hard time finding enough resources for serious study of China in the United States."

Nielsen ended the discussion on a pessimistic note about the fate of the humanities. "It is pretty clear that the humanities are really no more popular in foundation programs than they are in government programs. The Rockefeller Foundation, the Ford Foundation, the Mellon Foundation, the Volkswagen Foundation are really quite exceptional. The great majority of American foundations do not take any strong interest in the humanities, and I think, with the intensification of many of these social problems and the distress of many institutions—churches, hospitals, orphanages, services to the elderly, and so on—that the competition for funds is going to be the disadvantage of the humanities. For reasons that are very broad and deep, the humanities operate from a position of disadvantage and weakness in most of these funding competitions."

CORPORATE SUPPORT

The question which kinds of activities were most appropriate for different types of donors continued to dominate the ensuing discussions. Danella Schiffer of the Carnegie Corporation set the stage for a lively consideration of the appropriate parameters for corporate support of the humanities with the contention that humanists would have to present their case more coherently if they wished to receive corporate support for their activities. As Schiffer explained, many humanistic undertakings that need funding are not perceived as being relevant to the corporate interest and therefore compete poorly against other types of grant seekers. Nevertheless, she noted a growing awareness among U.S. businesses that liberal arts majors often make more successful employees than those with business or technical degrees, a finding which might make the corporate community more favorably disposed toward the humanities. Moreover, historians and philosophers are increasingly being used as consultants by companies. "Humanists have a chance to get corporations interested in preserving their disciplines," she concluded, but "it's going to be up to the humanists to develop that point."

In his commentary on Schiffer's presentation, Tadashi Yamamoto of the Japan Center for International Exchange outlined recent developments in Japanese corporate philanthropy and their implications for the humanities. As he explained, Japan's rapid economic growth, its rise to prominence in the international marketplace, and its businesspeople's desire to "improve their image and be better corporate citizens" contributed to the rise of corporate philanthropy in Japan during the 1970s. "Many of these foundations are interested in international activities, and particularly cooperative efforts in developing countries." They also have considerable leeway in giving to activities which "are not directly related to corporate interests," since many have independent boards of scholars and others conscripted from outside the corporation. As a result, they are "susceptible to good ideas. And if we exercise effective grantsmanship, I think they can be persuaded to identify needs in less directly beneficial fields, such as the humanities," particularly if they can be convinced that the welfare of the international community can be served by such endeavors. Thus, "if humanists can come up with more convincing arguments, and perhaps more effective packaging of their programs, Japanese corporations might be seduced."

Pointing to developments in Latin America, Enrique Fernandez of SOLIDARIOS in the Dominican Republic concurred that foreign corporate self-interest might be more muted than in the United States. "When a company sets up a foundation, it is precisely because it wants to avoid the involvement of corporate interest in foundation work. It wants its foundation to be as professional as possible in distributing funds." "Seduction" therefore depends upon the quality of the case, for "as long as whoever is going to conduct the program presents a well-thought-out case, this person will attract contributions."

Danella Schiffer was careful not to present too bright a picture of the U.S. scene, warning humanists not to "become too optimistic that support for the humanities will increase simply because corporate support is growing." For example, U.S. business giving "to the arts and culture is the fastest-growing area of corporate philanthropy in the United States, currently reaching about 11 percent. Yet many corporations think that they are supporting the humanities when they really are funding the arts." The confusion between the arts and the humanities is one of the major stumbling blocks to enhanced corporate support. If this situation is to change, "the humanities will have to change; they will have to redefine their mission. This is not the age of the Medici, with patrons who will support creative individuals because they are doing wonderful things. Humanistic scholarship will have to become more relevant to what is going on today."

Other participants found Schiffer's suggestions somewhat alarming and, to use Joel Colton's phrase, "not very convincing." Colton admitted that he was "very troubled" by her recommendations and countered her arguments by pointing out that the mere fact that businesses hire humanists is not enough to ensure "that there are good literature departments or philosophy departments." Nor did he see corporate employment of professionally trained humanists as a particularly promising sign. As he explained, the absorption of scholars into the corporate milieu "loses the humanist. The corporation takes an advanced humanist with a Ph.D. who spent a number of years in getting that degree, and then retrains him or her to be a manager. In the process, it provides a job for that person, but it doesn't really help the humanities. That person is lost to the humanities, except as a generalist who appreciates the humanities."

"How do you get humanists to redefine their mission?" Colton continued. "To ask humanists to redefine their mission in some profound way other than to say that they are engaged in a dialogue involving research and reflection about the human experience in all its variety, including business," is not necessarily legitimate. "I'm worried about redefining the humanities in some way that might cause them to lose their integrity, to disappear."

Ian Lancaster of Britain's Gulbenkian Foundation also admitted that he was seeing "some of those red lights that Joel Colton is seeing. I think that there is a danger, because of the growing financial might of corporations, particularly multinational corporations, that we may turn to them for financial support for the things which perhaps are not actually suitable for them to support, asking them to do things which go against their nature, and we may therefore risk that the applicant will do something against its nature. A balanced university needs to have a nuclear physics laboratory which might be appropriately supported by Westinghouse or GE. It also needs a strong department of philosophy and anthropology—that's what a university is, a place that embraces a great spectrum. It is necessary to identify which parts of the spectrum of learning are best suited to corporate support." In a more conciliatory vein, Lancaster conceded that humanists should appeal for corporate support, "but they need to do it knowingly and in ways which do not involve them in contorting themselves to fit somebody else's image. We have to ensure that we do not bend over too far backwards to get funding from the wrong sources."

Francis X. Sutton adopted a more moderate stance, drawing attention to the fact that there are some areas in which humanists and corporations are naturally allied. "I'm impressed with the fact that businesses are willing to spend money on the humanistic education of their executives," he noted. "The Aspen Institute is one of the great examples. More than $1 million per year is spent in fees by business corporations in order to send their executives to Aspen, in addition to grants made for Aspen's various activities in the humanities. The point is that there is an appreciation of the need for continuing personal development if people are to be effective corporate leaders."

W. McNeil Lowry also attempted to mediate between the two factions which were rapidly emerging. Rather than embarking upon a fundamental redefinition of their work, he suggested, perhaps humanists should explain "whatever relevance they might have more directly to the business community. I think that their record in this area is very poor." For example, "the importance of area studies is very poorly understood by most corporations, including those that benefit directly from such studies. The information that comes out of area studies about various parts of the world is of as much use to government and corporations as to the scholars themselves. And this does not contort the activities of the scholars. This is exactly what they want to do. But they don't tell it very well, and they don't tell it to the right people. And the corporations have to hear it."

Danella Schiffer enthusiastically concurred. Rather than shifting the nature of their activities, "humanists have to do a better job of making themselves understood." As she explained, this does not necessarily mean that they have to change what they do; what has to be changed is "how they relate it to everyday life."

OPTIMISTS AND PESSIMISTS

Little consensus was ultimately reached on a prognosis for future support for the humanities at the governmental, corporate, or private foundation level. As the discussions progressed, the participants increasingly sorted themselves into optimists who applauded the public's growing appetite for noninstitutional educational schemes and pessimists who bemoaned the declining fortunes of humanistic study within academe. These divisions were sharpened, in part, by the Americans' insistence that the humanities and social sciences remain distinctly separated, an idea foreign to many of the non-American participants. "This is a particularly American problem," explained Malcolm Richardson of the Rockefeller Foundation, for "Europeans distinguish principally between natural sciences and the study of man, or *sciences humaines,* whereas Americans are more likely to draw a sharp boundary between science of every sort and the humanities."

Joel Colton's comments on the "problem of how to enhance the role of the humanities in contemporary society" brought the two lines of argument into sharper focus:

We do not live in a world that is favorable to the humanities, despite many popular signs. The Humanities Commission Report pointed out that more people in the United States went to visit museums and concerts than went to athletic events. But that is not the same as taking up a book and studying it. We are present-minded, and we like action rather than contemplation. People working in foundations tend to be practical-minded people of affairs, who work with trustees who are even more action-minded. But our world would be very different without the people who cultivate and nurture the study of humanistic topics such as history, philosophy, and literature. I think that even government, business, and foundation people would admit that. The question is a question of priorities, of limited resources. With worldwide inflation, what can we ask people to do? In some ways we have a custodial role to play in nurturing cultural inquiry, in the sense that we have to help preserve and safeguard the best, whether through our libraries and museums or through educational institutions. It is sometimes said that the humanities are perceived as useless subjects, and so it is very difficult to get foundations to support them unless you have some selling points.

Other participants were quick to challenge Colton's concern. Francis X. Sutton led the "optimist" charge, attacking the "sad tone that seems to center around too much discussion of the humanities." Noting that he found this attitude "a little puzzling when it is combined with this extraordinary interest in the arts, this searching for cultural experience which is so characteristic of the contemporary world," Sutton argued that "the humanities are escaping the academy. The academy is only a small part of the cultural enterprise that goes on, and we need to perceive the whole enterprise in its variety and continuity, rather than just as an exercise in scholarship."

In order to bolster his position, Sutton cited the example of the Beaubourg Museum in Paris, which "has more visitors than the Eiffel Tower and more than Versailles. There are more visitors there than there are at the Smithsonian, which is the most-attended museum in the United States. This is a humanistic enterprise. People walk along listening to speeches by the gallery lecturers. They get all sorts of information. They obviously exchange comments with one another, and they read the newspapers about what is going on there. This sort of commentary and reaction is a humanistic enterprise, and it is enormously expanded and active in the modern world." Museum exhibitions "are of extraordinary importance for understanding the great social variety in the world." The Nigeria show, the King Tut show, and similar events "foster important perceptions that we previously have not had. The breadth and depth of understanding that you gain in visiting one of these things becomes the kind of stimulus that most of us need. And they contribute considerably to the understanding of other areas and cultures."

Others remained unconvinced. Sutton's former colleague, W. McNeil Lowry, attacked what he termed the "temporary fads" embodied in many of these activities, the "reduction of art to a passing show." As Lowry noted, "Such activities are not necessarily indicative of the aesthetic, moral, or philosophical values of a society."

Joel Colton took up Lowry's point, emphasizing the distinction between the arts and humanities. "We cannot merely think of the public outreach that involves going to museums and watching productions on television," he cautioned. "We have to think of the humanities as in some way having to do with scholarship. It has something to do with thinking about the tradition relating to the human experience. You can name a number of disciplines—history and literature and philosophy and languages—in which there are very serious problems—very serious. Enrollments in these subjects have declined. Professional opportunities for highly trained people who have as much training as any M.D. do not exist. So in a sense this is what we have to think about when we think about the humanities."

After conceding that "the arts have a certain appeal in our society, whether they have the appeal of a passer through or something more profound," Colton deftly shifted the discussion back to the humanities. "How many of you would feel," he queried, "that in the disciplined study of subjects like history, literature, philosophy, language, there is reason for pessimism in your own country? Has there been a decline in the students' interest? Are they majoring in practical, preprofessional subjects when they go to a college in the hopes of getting into law schools or graduate schools of business? What is happening to people who are training themselves to become teachers—are there fewer opportunities for them? Is there a reason for the pessimism, in your experience, in your own countries?"

Ian Lancaster took up the refrain, adding his voice to the pessimist camp by drawing attention to the anti-intellectual opposition to secular humanism brewing in the United States. "On the basis of the experience in Britain and in the United States at the moment," he noted, "the real cause for pessimism is the attack on education in the broadest sense. Whether it is only a result of economic factors, or whether it reflects some other backlash against education, is difficult to say."

Lowry agreed, pointing out that in the United States, humanistic study has "been equated within an antitheological, atheistic tradition by people who want to attack it on that basis because they're not really concerned about it as a philosophical system. They wish to attack tolerance, to impose censorship in libraries, in secondary school courses, and so they attack humanism as a godless heresy." Enlarging upon one of the themes of his presentation, Lowry emphasized that "the essence of the humanities is the ability to make choices. It is that operation of choice which is the basis of scholarship." As a result, "there are attitudes and values underlying the humanities that conflict with many tendencies in our society, and there are many tendencies in our society that conflict with the humanities. But these are attacks on the higher educational system itself, and not simply on the humanities."

Undeterred, Sutton asked, "May I keep up my optimism?" He then proceeded to dissect the major tenets of the pessimist camp. As he explained, after an initial rush of "extraordinary expansion" in the postwar decades, "there is now a period of worldwide retrenchment, disillusionment, and heavy unemployment among educated people at all levels, which we are going to have to face for a considerable time." As a result, "there is now a tendency to react to the exaggerated optimism of a couple of decades after the Second World War with a period of great pessimism." Nevertheless, he continued,

> the consequences of that extraordinary upsurge in education around the world in the postwar years are very hopeful for civilization and the humanities because there are so many more educated people, and this produces needs which go on throughout long lifetimes. We must not think of the need for humanistic education as something that is confined to the period when people are in college. The number of people who are taking degrees in the humanities is not an adequate measure of the interest in the humanities in the world nowadays. People are trying to make something interesting of their lives as they go along. Moreover, it seems quite natural that in a period of high unemployment there should be a move toward vocationalism and useful degrees. Nor does this seem to me to be something that need give us terrible concern about the state of cultural and humanistic interest in the society. That continues to grow in the bleak period that we are now in. And it seems to me that the basis for a real efflorescence of humanistic interest is there.

Lancaster demurred, urging the conferees not to "mistake comprehensiveness for depth." Casual exposure to cultural programs is not enough to ensure an educated citizenry, much less the continued viability of the humanities. "The problem at the moment," he explained, "is that television and newspapers often substitute for books and learning. . . . One of the key factors that we have to be concerned with is that aspect of the humanities which is concerned with understanding in depth, seeing below the surface, getting into fundamental issues, in a way that television cannot do. The more the technological media come to play a part in people's lives, the greater the schism between breadth and depth of knowledge will be."

Gideon Paz of the America-Israel Cultural Foundation agreed. "When I was in New York," he recalled, "people were standing in line to have a glimpse at the Mona Lisa, but I do not know that this is a sign of involvement with the arts. Certainly, public access to information is much wider than it was before, but the depth of learning is much lower."

Wolfgang Heisenberg of Germany's Thyssen Foundation added a third voice to this line of reasoning. As he explained, "I have serious doubts that the more than one million people who saw the King Tut exhibit in Cologne have a real understanding of these objects as objects of art. They see them as sensational and queer, certainly interesting artifacts, but extremely difficult to understand as art objects."

Danella Schiffer introduced another concern, reiterating caveats voiced in the earlier discussions. "I think we ought to be pessimistic about funding possibilities, or at least guardedly so," she noted; "I would suggest that the problem may rest with the humanists themselves. In the United States, for example, the humanities are often perceived as being irrelevant to modern life, to modern society. If we want to preserve the humanities, we have to start thinking about how we can talk about them to the general public, because the general public will determine the fate of the humanities in the future."

Enrique Fernandez concurred, stressing the need to "promote a dialogue between specialists in the humanities and those who are not specialists." As he explained, this approach is particularly necessary in the Third World. "People in developed societies have solved their basic human problems, and so they can afford to worry about the humanities. People in the Third World, on the other hand, are still fighting for their day-to-day human needs." As a result, a better case has to be made for the relevance of cultural activity to basic concerns in developing nations.

Tadashi Yamamoto adopted the mediator's role. Noting the "crosscurrents between the popularized forms of the humanities and the more disciplinary kind of thing," Yamamoto predicted that government funding for humanistic study would continue at the same level in Japan, but expressed doubt that "most of these fields are capable of addressing contemporary issues in any meaningful way." He also blamed "specialists in the humanities for their failure to relate better to people outside their disciplines." Television production, for example, "can be improved by cooperation with specialists in the humanities," but "just downgrading the superficiality of TV productions" is unrealistic and unproductive. Echoing the sentiments of Schiffer and Fernandez, Yamamoto stressed the needs and "opportunities for people in the humanities to have a dialogue with people on the outside."

Henry Cavanna of the Fondation Internationale des Sciences Humaines in France posited a compelling case for the humanities. He eloquently countered his fellow conferees' doubts about the relevance of cultural inquiry to contemporary concerns by underscoring the inherent relationship between the humanities and the social sciences, for "the social sciences are the sciences in which all of us try to find solutions to problems of poverty, equality, social security, and related issues. . . . It is impossible to have very good sociology, for instance, unless you know history, because what is sociology but trying to discover human laws of behavior?" History gives insight into human behavior and the forces governing that behavior over the long term. Literature is also important: "So much has been said about psychoanalysis over the last twenty or thirty years. But if you go back to the classics, you will see that practically all important characters and psychological issues have already been studied and described in the Greek classics, by Shakespeare, Cervantes, Goethe, and others. There is direct relevance."

"Or," Cavanna continued, "take the problem of power," a central concern of social scientific inquiry. Contemporary science has "discovered the means of destroying mankind. How are we going to solve this problem? The use of power is a problem of ethics. Philosophical considerations of these issues are very important." Religious studies also have contemporary relevance: "Is it possible to believe that a society which has no religion whatsoever will solve its problems in the same way as a religiously oriented society? Whether or not you are a believer, it is quite clear from a purely sociological standpoint that a society which does not believe in an afterlife will try to solve all problems of equality, power, and fulfillment in this world. But if you believe in an afterlife, it is quite clear that the solution is going to be different." Through religion, ethics, history, the classics, and literature, he noted, we can understand social science problems more clearly.

CONCLUSION

The preliminary round of discussions was, to use Ian Lancaster's phrase, "unashamedly American" in content and focus. Several important issues were raised. The conferees expressed both optimism and pessimism over the fate of the humanities, revealing a variety of attitudes about the proper focus for foundation funding. Led by Francis X. Sutton and Raymond Georis of the European Cultural Foundation, the optimist camp cast its nets widely to include museum outreach and media events. In the process, the people in this group displayed a deeply humane faith in individual perfectibility and the lifelong search for culture, a stance which was rejected by their more academically minded opponents. Proponents of the pessimist point of view questioned the sophistication of outreach efforts and underscored the superficiality of many museum programs and media events. Others expressed doubts about the relevance of humanistic endeavor to contemporary concerns—criticism neatly countered by Henry Cavanna's eloquent statement about the mesh between humanistic inquiry and the social sciences. The need for better dialogue among scholars, governments, funders, and the larger community was a recurrent theme, as was suitability. Both government and corporate support were surveyed and found wanting. In some instances, the appropriateness of such support for humanistic enterprises was questioned; in others, the scope and future of these types of funding were at issue.

The overall impression generated by these discussions was one of expanding opportunities for humanistic education outside the academy and dwindling resources within; of corporate expansion, governmental retrenchment, and growing uncertainty among private foundations. In the end, little consensus was reached on the fate of the humanities, and the very absence of agreement suggests that it is indeed the best and worst of times for cultural endeavors.

PART TWO

The International Scene

INTRODUCTION

Although foundations are generally perceived as American phenomena, modern grant-making organizations now operate throughout the world. The essays and discussions in this part examine the extent of these developments and their implications for the humanities, and provide vignettes of contemporary policies and trends in Western Europe, Japan, and the Third World. Several issues previously examined in an American context are reassessed from an international perspective, including public/private relationships and prospects for cultural largesse.

The discussions which centered on the Third World were particularly animated. While some of the participants eloquently defended cultural activities in underdeveloped nations, others expressed keen doubts about the propriety of such efforts in areas still racked by endemic social and economic ills. The discussions repeatedly emphasized the need to work in concert with local scholars and policy makers and often raised issues markedly critical of earlier U.S. efforts, criticisms which were parried by the programs' architects. The papers and discussions reveal many areas of shared concern, tentative collaboration, and critical disagreement among the world's funders, vividly underscoring the inherent problems of, and prospects for, worldwide foundation cooperation.

6 / Non-U.S. Foundations: An Overview

KATHLEEN D. McCARTHY

Americans tend to adopt a myopically ethnocentric attitude about foundations. However, as this essay points out, foundation philanthropy has become increasingly internationalized since the Second World War. Concentrations of modern foundations may now be found throughout Western Europe and Japan and in some areas of Latin America, Asia, and the Middle East. Kathleen D. McCarthy explores the historical roots of these developments, comparing non-U.S. foundations to their U.S. counterparts, and weighs the implications of these trends for cultural inquiry and exchange.

Contemporary observers often question whether the philanthropic impulse can flourish, much less survive, outside the United States. During the 1970s, critics argued that foreign philanthropy was going out of style, crippled by stringent tax laws, leftist critiques, and the rise of the welfare state. As Waldemar Nielsen explained, "European governments offer[ed] few inducements and many impediments to would-be donors." Few new funds were being created, and those which did exist "exist[ed] in name only, making only minimal outlays." In effect, private charity had "quite gone out of favor" beyond American shores.[1]

Yet recent statistics reveal that, far from sounding the death knell for foundations, the postwar decades witnessed the birth of a new international philanthropic order. Over 50 percent of the European foundations listed in the Agnelli Foundation directory were established since 1950; 79 percent of those cited in the Russell Sage Foundation's study of Latin American giving were created after 1951; and in both instances the numbers have been rising.[2] Scores of modern foundations have been initiated in Japan within the last decade alone. Even in stubbornly resistant nations such as France, efforts are now under way to revamp existing laws and tax provisions to encourage the development of private foundations. In light of these developments, it is important to understand why these foundations were created, how they compare to their U.S. counterparts, and what impact their activities have had within specific programmatic areas, such as the humanities.

Although proportions vary considerably betweeen nations, the complex American mix of public, private, corporate, family, and individual largesse has been partially replicated outside the United States. Many of the best-known and most active foreign organizations—including the Aga Khan, Juan March, Calouste Gulbenkian, and Eugenio Mendoza foundations—bear the names of individual donors.[3] Others were created by families, particularly in India, where foundations tend to cluster around the fortunes of a few socially conscious industrialist clans such as the Tatas in Bombay, the Birlas in Calcutta, and the Sarabhais in Ahmedabad.[4]

In a loose parallel to American trends, corporations are often important donors. U.S. corporate philanthropy dates from the nineteenth century, when businesses first supported YMCAs for the benefit of their employees. World War I and the rise of community chests in the 1920s broadened the scope and magnitude of U.S. business giving, while the Internal Revenue Service Act of 1936 and the favorable Supreme Court ruling in the *Smith* v. *Barlow* case (1953) provided the legal underpinnings, enabling businesses to donate up to 5 percent of their pretax net earnings to charitable ends.[5]

Most non-U.S. corporate foundations are of more recent origin. Venezuelan business philanthropy began to develop in the 1950s, when oil companies such as Creole Petroleum (1956) and Shell (1959) took advantage of oil profits and enlightened tax legislation to establish grant-making agencies.[6] Corporate foundations were also slow to take root in Japan, discouraged by the lack of a strong tradition of organized philanthropy and the pervasive role of the state, which assumed responsibility for the provision of most health, welfare, and educational services. The Japanese government continues to play a major role not only in this respect but in the regulation of those seeking to provide such services through private means. Foundation activities are subject to public regulation and supervision, and the ministry responsible for this function varies with the institution's programmatic interests, so that the development of multipurpose foundations is extremely complicated. Charters are granted at the discretion of public officials, and methods of inspection differ widely. No single set of laws or standards currently regulates governmental activities in the private sector. Tax incentives are also quite limited and uneven. Most Japanese foundations are corporate, rather than private, ventures, since the laws do not permit extensive deductions for individual charitable contributions and militate against the creation of sizable personal foundations. Nor are corporate donations completely unfettered. Businesses are denied deductions for grants made outside the country and to fields other than science and technology.

Despite these drawbacks, Japanese philanthropy has flourished, aided by the encouragement and assistance of the Japanese Philanthropy Project of the Japan Center for International Exchange (JCIE).[7] Thousands of charitable corporations were created during the 1970s alone, and although most are still relatively small by U.S. standards, prospects for their continued expansion seem promising.

Several factors helped to nurture these developments. Japanese corporations inspired a swelling chorus of criticism during the 1970s for their perceived role in fostering worldwide trade imbalances, environmental pollution, and inflationary trends. Corporate largesse is one means by which Japanese businessmen may publicly demonstrate their willingness to shoulder a measure of responsibility for redressing the domestic and international ills which have accompanied rapid modernization. Ideally, such activities will also stimulate mutual understanding and cooperation in key market areas, mute lingering wartime antipathies, raise the standard of living, and forge fresh links among the world's intellectual, political, and business elites.[8]

Donors in Japan and elsewhere have also launched regranting agencies akin to U.S. community trusts. The community trust idea originated in the United States in the 1910s as a means of redressing the problem of outmoded charitable endowments, facilitating the ongoing modernization of donors' gifts, providing clearinghouses for new philanthropic ideas, managing individual endowments, and actively encouraging the creation of new foundations. This model has proved particularly well suited to nations such as France and Japan, where both the Asian Community Trust (1979) and the Fondation de France (1969) have been developed along American lines.[9]

Governments, too, occasionally create private, or quasi-private foundations, such as Germany's Volkswagen Foundation. A publicly initiated private grant maker, Volkswagen was created through a treaty between the governments of Lower Saxony and the Federal Republic of Germany in order to settle the disputed ownership of the Volkswagenwerk in 1961. Similarly, the Swedish Riksdag established the Bank of Sweden Tercentenary Foundation in 1962, and the Japanese Diet founded the quasi-private Japan Foundation a decade later.[10]

Precedents for such activities are more deeply ingrained in some countries than in others. The legitimation of foundation philanthropy tends to proceed at a laggardly pace in traditional societies where little excess cash is available for such activities, and charity is carried out within the sequestered arena of family, community, and kin. Communist nations have frowned on private beneficence in all its forms, including foundations. Governmental and legal impediments have also slowed foundation diffusion in industrial democracies such as France, where state hostility toward individual social action still lingers as a legacy of the Revolution. The Latin American situation has been similarly hampered by governmental indifference, spiraling inflation, and the pervasiveness of the Code Napoléon, which makes no provision for the development of charitable trusts.

Ample precedents, many of which are religiously inspired, abound in other parts of the world. Almsgiving is considered one of the fundamental duties of the devout in Islamic states, where philanthropic activities are characterized by the development of *waqfs* (religious trusts), some of which have recently begun to adopt more modern aims and techniques under the combined pressures of urbanization, oil money, examples of innovative leaders such as the Aga Khan, and the Middle East's sudden rise to world stature. The Judeo-Christian ethic also stresses tithing and service to the poor, traditions which are readily translated into foundation programs.

Protestant nations are generally regarded as more fertile ground for such activities than Catholic countries, where giving is funneled through the church. In England, for example, the Elizabethan Statute of Charitable Uses, drafted in 1601 in response to conditions triggered by the Protestant Reformation, is still in use today.[11] Germany has a comparably rich tradition of private philanthropy. Almost 100,000 trusts were operating by the 1910s, including such giants as the Carl Zeiss and Krupp foundations; 90 percent of these trusts subsequently faltered, however, undermined by war, inflation, and endemic monetary devaluations. The philanthropic order revived with Hitler's passing, spurred by new enabling legislation and the Federal Republic's reassumption of power among the world's industrial and economic leaders. Four thousand German grant-making agencies were operating by 1975, and their numbers were estimated to be increasing at a rate of approximately fifty each year.

The dissemination and internationalization of the foundation movement have been facilitated, in part, by governmental initiatives. Austrian authorities liberalized that nation's charitable trust laws in 1975, the Finnish government endorsed the creation of new foundations in 1977, and legal revisions in Sweden exempting certain kinds of contributions from income and gift taxes attest to a more favorable view of foundations since World War II. Similarly, hundreds of small private and corporate foundations developed in Turkey after the passage of Law 903 (1967), which granted tax immunity to agencies reducing burdens on the public till.[12]

Citizen efforts have played a comparably significant role. One of the founders of the Fondation de France, Conseil d'Etat member Michel Pomey, was a leader in the campaign to liberalize the charitable tax laws in order to encourage French grant-making initiatives. The Japanese, too, have vigorously lobbied for lighter tax burdens. In 1981, for example, the U.S.–Japan Economic Relations Group submitted a report to the president of the United States and the Japanese prime minister requesting additional tax incentives for Japanese donors to international nonprofit organizations.

Differences between U.S. and foreign systems should not be minimized, however. While the American tradition of voluntarism is deeply rooted in the nation's past and has proved resistant to extensive governmental regulation, other countries have not fared as well. Many nations, including Japan, Spain, France, Italy, Portugal, Austria, and Germany, require official sanction for the creation of new foundations. Once they are initiated, public surveillance of their activities is often far more rigorous than in the United States. Nor do many countries provide tax incentives comparable to those of the United States. In France, for example, citizens are allowed scant charitable deductions of 1–5 percent (as opposed to 20–30 percent in the United States), and charitable bequests cannot be made without the heirs' consent. As a result, most gifts are rendered *inter vivos*. Thus, antithetical state controls, tax laws, and public attitudes, as well as endemic inflation and the ravages of war, often slow the growth of individual fortunes and foundation philanthropy outside the United States.[13]

Although the grant-making capacities of giants like the Volkswagen and Gulbenkian foundations compare favorably to those of Rockefeller, Carnegie, and Ford, most U.S. and foreign foundations are more modestly endowed. According to Foundation Center statistics, as of 1980 only 47 of America's 22,000 foundations had assets of $100 million or more; 895 were capitalized at $5 million to $50 million; but over half (11,445) had endowments of less than $1 million.[14] Tables 1 and 2 give a sense of how some of the non-U.S. foundations mentioned in this essay compare in size to leading corporate grant makers in the United States.

Table 1.   SELECTED NON-U.S. FOUNDATIONS

Foundation	Country	Assets	(year)	Budget	(year)
Volkswagen	Germany	$513,939,000	(1976)	$35,714,285	(1976)
Gulbenkian	Portugal	325,427,900	(1976)	20,786,100	(1976)
Bank of Sweden Tercentenary Fund	Sweden	91,212,720	(1980)	5,832,765	(1980)
Fritz Thyssen	Germany	65,158,626	(1976)	5,033,783	(1976)
Wolfson	England	60,000,000	(1976)	5,000,000	(1976)
Hoso Bunka	Japan	52,610,000	(1980)		
Toyota	Japan	43,480,000	(1980)		
Nuffield	England	32,168,563	(1976)	3,294,927	(1976)
Mitsubishi	Japan	19,570,000	(1980)		
Agnelli	Italy	7,500,000	(1977)	1,100,000	(1977)
Fondation de France	France	5,000,000	(1980)		
Mendoza	Venezuela	4,000,000	(1977)	1,100,000	(1978)
Leverhulme Trust	England			3,366,000	(1976)
Kajima	Japan	3,260,000	(1980)		
Turkish Education Foundation	Turkey	2,840,000	(1976)		
Development Foundation of Turkey	Turkey			1,768,653	(1976)
Shell	Venezuela			1,426,628	(1972)
Boulton	Venezuela			100,000	(1977)

Table 2. LARGEST U.S. CORPORATE FOUNDATIONS, 1979

Foundation	Budget
Ford Motor Company Fund	$13,669,446
Exxon Education Foundation	13,493,347
Atlantic Richfield Foundation	13,116,853
General Motors Foundation	13,052,836
Mobil Foundation, Inc.	7,432,020
Dayton Hudson Foundation	7,080,287
BankAmerica Foundation	7,055,711
Alcoa Foundation	6,773,829
United States Steel Foundation, Inc.	6,441,329
Monsanto Fund	6,415,279
Amoco Foundation, Inc.	6,012,064
Proctor and Gamble Fund	5,975,424
Shell Companies Foundation, Inc.	5,799,505
General Mills Foundation	5,576,274
Eastman Kodak Charitable Trust	4,952,369
General Electric Foundation	4,878,921
Western Electric Fund	4,835,545
Gulf Oil Foundation of Delaware	4,575,895
Prudential Foundation	4,214,992
Aetna Life and Casualty Foundation	4,157,560
Minnesota Mining and Manufacturing Foundation, Inc.	3,914,030

Source: Foundation Center data base.

Several attempts have recently been made to coordinate the activities of non-U.S. foundations and their American counterparts in order to promote international cooperation and information exchange. In 1981 a conference in Caracas, Venezuela, brought together U.S. and Latin American foundation representatives to discuss programs, procedures, and staffing techniques, and SOLIDARIOS has current plans for a follow-up meeting in the Dominican Republic in 1985.[15] Other efforts include the Japanese Philanthropy Project, which brings together European, American, and Japanese foundation spokesmen; the Hague Club (a group of European foundation executives who meet informally to discuss issues of mutual interest and concern); the Council on Foundations' Committee for International Grantmakers; and Interphil, a loosely structured coalition headquartered in Europe. Multinational compendia like the Agnelli Foundation directory also track foundation initiatives, helping to keep members of the funding community apprised of foreign trends.

Despite these centralizing efforts, however, reliable data about specific programmatic areas remain difficult, if not impossible, to obtain. This situation is particularly acute in fields such as the humanities, and it is exacerbated by the fact that the distinctions among the arts, the humanities, and the social sciences, so insistently sharp in the United States, are irrelevant or blurred elsewhere. What little available information exists suggests that a minority of non-U.S. foundations devote significant amounts to domestic or international cultural activities. Contributions to the humanities are clearly dwarfed by funding for scientific, technical, and development projects.[16]

In Australia, only five trusts support humanistic enterprises, accounting for only 1.5 percent of the nation's grant-making total for 1979. By contrast, private grants to the arts leveled off at 5.5 percent and those to human welfare activities at 39.5 percent.[17] Few Latin American organizations underwrite humanistic research or even sporadically fund projects on a par with the edition of Venezuelan classics sponsored by Fundación Shell in the 1960s. European foundations echo the same pattern. The Fondation de France's Paul Valéry Prize for Literature, awarded to French historians and literary figures of national renown, is only a minor component in the foundation's overall program. The Agnelli Foundation's recently published history of Italian art and culture,[18] the Bank of Sweden Tercentenary Foundation's equal opportunity program, the Gulbenkian Foundation's literary translations, and the Leverhulme Trust's institutional and research grants represent other significant, but limited, programs (see Table 3).

German foundations rank among the leading European donors to the humanities. A survey conducted by the National Endowment for the Humanities estimated that German foundations donated a respectable $6,370,000 to humanistic projects in 1970, although as in the case of American foundations, any figure is necessarily impressionistic. The Volkswagen and Thyssen foundations have particularly important domestic and international programs in the social sciences and humanities, promoting institutional development and scholarly cooperation both in Germany and abroad.[19] Volkswagen's domestic programs range from "History and Science, and Technology" to "Research on Cultural Heritage," encompassing a broad schema of scholarly research, conferences, symposia, and archival, museum, and library devel-

Table 3. SELECTED FOREIGN FOUNDATION GRANTS
FOR CULTURAL RESEARCH

England—Leverhulme Trust (1981 grants)

University of Kent, Canterbury:	research for bibliography of 18th-century legal literature
Keston College, Kent:	research for study of developments in the Russian Orthodox church, 1969–80
University of London, University College:	preparation of a new translation of the Domesday Book
University of Glasgow:	research on historical thesaurus of English
University of Cambridge:	research for study of Oriental and African music and its performance

Sweden—The Bank of Sweden Tercentenary Foundation (1981 grants)

University of Stockholm:	Women and Social Change: A Social Anthropological Study of Women's Participation in Social and Economic Change in Five Different Societies (research project)
Uppsala University:	Language and Sex (research project)
University of Gothenberg:	Society and Prostitution in Sweden, 1812–1918 (research project)
Stockholm University:	Women's Work in Swedish Industry, 1810–1920 (research project)
University of Uppsala:	Family Limitation in Sweden, 1870–1935: The Changing Attitudes of Women, the Family, and Society (research project)

Japan—Toyota Foundation (1980–81 grants)

Sri Nakarinwirot University, Thailand:	southern Thai dictionary compilation
Padjadjaran University, Indonesia:	inventory and recording of Sundanese manuscripts
Silpakorn University, Thailand:	history of Southeast Asian architecture
Silpakorn University, Thailand:	the structure of northern Thai mural paintings
Chulalongkorn University, Thailand:	linguistic variations in the speech of selected communities in Thailand

Table 3. SELECTED FOREIGN FOUNDATION GRANTS
FOR CULTURAL RESEARCH—*Continued*

Germany—The Volkswagen Foundation (1980 areas of interest)

Contemporary studies in South-
east Asia
Comparative European history
North American studies
Contemporary studies in the Near
and Middle East
Contemporary studies in Eastern
Europe
History of humanities, science,
and technology—Germany
Research on cultural heritage

opment. The foundation's budget allocates 5–10 percent of its expenditures for foreign applicants, including researchers in Southeast Asia, Europe, North America, and the Near and Middle East. This research fosters scholarship on contemporary issues and promotes intellectual interchange between European and foreign scholars.

Despite the fact that donations for such activities are not tax exempt, a small number of Japanese foundations also fund international cultural ventures. One of the most innovative initiatives is Toyota's "Know Our Neighbors" Translation-Publication Program. Toyota's staff has labored since 1977 to develop contacts throughout Southeast Asia for cultural preservation and revitalization programs. To date, these projects have included such diverse activities as the microfilming of ancient Thai manuscripts, the publication of language dictionaries, and research on traditional architecture. The "Know Our Neighbors" program, which was initiated in 1978, translates major literary works from Singapore, Thailand, Malaysia, Burma, the Philippines, and Indonesia into Japanese. Before embarking upon the program, Toyota polled more than a hundred leading Southeast Asian scholars and professionals for ideas about the project and suggestions of possible works for translation. Since its inception, more than thirty-one Southeast Asian works have been translated and made available in Japan.

Of course, innovative, privately funded programs such as this account for only a small fraction of the money invested in cultural research. In Germany, for example, the publicly financed Deutsches Forschungsgemeinschaft (DFG, founded in 1949) is the primary backer of the humanities, supporting individual and team research projects, university research centers, and travel and publication costs. In Japan the Agency for Cultural Affairs of the Ministry of Education funds cultural preservation, dissemination, and development at home, while the Japan Foundation fulfills the same role abroad.

Even the governments of less-developed countries have begun to assume a growing share of responsibility for cultural preservation and humanities research. India's National Culture Trust includes the Academy of Art (1954); the Academy of Drama, Dance and Music (1953); the Academy of Letters (1957), which fosters multilingual activity; and the National Book Trust (1957), which funds, publishes, and disseminates classical Indian works. Similarly, Malaysia's Cultural Research Division (1972) and Burma's Department of Ancient Literature and Culture are heavily involved in cultural preservation and literary, museum, and research activities. In Asia, as in Europe and Latin America, public rather than private largesse supports the bulk of cultural endeavor.

Yet the worldwide economic recession has forced many of these governmental agencies to reduce their budgets and thus has cast private donors in a new role. The shifting balance of responsibility is vividly reflected in the annual reports of U.S. and foreign foundations. As Meriel Wilmot of Australia's Myer Foundation explains, U.S., British, and Australian foundations have traditionally viewed their mission as one of filling gaps left by the government. In recent years, "the so-called gaps [have] become ravines." The implications for foundations are immediate and starkly etched, for they "are now under considerable social pressure to support people and programmes which in the past ten years had been seen almost solely as government responsibilities."[20]

In Britain, Nuffield Foundation spokespersons have echoed Miss Wilmot's concern, noting that "in past years, when the Foundation made grants for experimental action, rather than research, it was in the expectation that at the end of the grant period the project, if successful, would be financed by central or local governments. It is no longer possible to make any such assumption and foundations which make grants of that sort now have to give serious consideration to the possibility that projects will close down at the end of the experimental period, perhaps leaving a local community without a resource on which it has come to rely."[21] Private grant-making agencies are now being asked to supply operating support, "to devote a larger part of our resources than before simply to sustain in action worthwhile enterprises, threatened with extinction by economic cuts."[22] The dilemma is, of course, not entirely worldwide. Areas such as Japan experienced cuts in public expenditures more slowly than the United States and parts of Western Europe. Nevertheless, the shifting balance of responsibility between public and private donors is fast becoming an issue of growing concern both in the United States and abroad.

Whether governmental reverses will ultimately give substance to the claims of gloomy Jeremiahs who predict the decline of international philanthropy remains to be seen. If they are correct, the combined weight of economic reverses, endemic inflation, competing domestic needs, and popular disillusionment with foreign aid will ultimately curb the growth of international largesse. Although hard data remain to be gathered, most foreign grant makers appear to have opted for programs grounded in science, social welfare, health, development, and agricultural reform, many of which are directed toward domestic ends. One of the most compelling tasks of the next decades will be to accrue better information on the scope and focus of foreign foundation work and on the relationship of these activities to governmental funding.

It appears clear that the foundation movement itself is destined to grow. In Europe, Latin America, Asia, and the Middle East modern foundations, frequently based on U.S. models and occasionally developed with U.S. aid, have taken root in what is often decidedly inhospitable soil. The foundation ideal has been exported and honed to fit the specific contours of indigenous traditions and needs. Despite the fact that few countries match U.S. tax incentives, individuals, families, corporations, and even governments have created significant grant-making organizations in recent years. In Moslem and Anglo-Saxon nations long-standing attitudes about public stewardship have nurtured these trends. In other areas, most notably, Latin America, France, and Japan, modern foundations have begun to develop in the absence of traditional sanctions. Like their corporate counterparts in the United States, many of these fledgling organizations are small; they are thus logical locations for the development of modestly scaled, carefully crafted

programs like Toyota's "Know Our Neighbors" project, to counterpoint the sweeping ventures of giants like UNESCO and Ford.
What these trends will mean for specific areas such as the humanities remains to be seen. What is certain is that the ensuing decades
will mark a watershed in the course of international philanthropy
as individuals, corporations, and governments reassess their roles,
rights, and responsibilities toward the public weal.

NOTES

1. Waldemar A. Nielsen, *The Endangered Sector* (New York: Columbia
University Press, 1979), pp. 234–35.
2. *Guide to European Foundations* (Turin: Fondazione Giovanni
Agnelli, 1978); Ann Stromberg, ed., *Philanthropic Foundations in Latin
America* (New York: Russell Sage Foundation, 1968).
3. Founded in 1967 by the forty-ninth hereditary imam of the Ismaili
Moslems, a sect of fifteen million adherents spread across twenty-five
countries, the Aga Khan Foundation has promoted a variety of health,
educational, and social welfare concerns throughout the developing world.
Some of its most recent projects include the Aga Khan Hospital in
Karachi, Pakistan, and the recently opened Aga Khan University; a string
of rural health centers throughout India and Pakistan; the Aga Khan
Medical Center in Kisumu, Kenya; health research in Bangladesh; an
international scholarship program based in Geneva; and grants to the
Institute of Islamic Studies at McGill University. The foundation is based
in Geneva, with branch offices in Bangladesh, Canada, India, Kenya,
Pakistan, and London. For additional information, see the Aga Khan
Foundation *Annual Report* and its brochure entitled *Some Current Projects*, January 1983.
Founded in Spain in 1955, the Juan March Foundation was the creation of the reputed billionaire Juan March, who was generally believed
to be that country's richest citizen after World War II. March, a staunch
supporter of General Franco during the Spanish Civil War, was a financial genius who controlled the nation's tobacco and gasoline monopolies
and many of its banking, brewery, chemical, and steel companies. Labeled
everything from "the Rockefeller of Spain" to "the last pirate of the
Mediterranean," March died in an automobile accident in 1962, leaving
a total of $33 million in bequests and *inter vivos* gifts for his foundation.
Among its many programs, the Juan March Foundation supports cultural
projects in Spain and abroad.
Calouste Gulbenkian was born an Armenian, lived in Portugal, carried
British citizenship, and commanded a fortune based on Iraqi oil. Born
the son of a rich merchant-banker in Constantinople in 1869, Gulbenkian studied engineering in London before embarking on his business

career. The foundation which bears his name reflects the oilman's passion for art, as well as his interest in Portuguese and Armenian welfare. At present, the Gulbenkian Foundation operates a Portuguese Cultural Center in Paris; a British branch devoted to social welfare, education, and the arts; and a variety of charitable, artistic, educational, and scientific programs funded through its headquarters in Lisbon. Some of its more humanistically oriented programs include a nationwide traveling library program; translations and publications of important cultural works; and support of a variety of Portuguese studies programs and fellowships. As of 1975, the Gulbenkian Foundation's assets were estimated to be in excess of $433 million.

Eugenio Mendoza's philanthropic activities, which spanned more than three decades, have helped to spark the creation of a variety of Venezuelan foundations, beginning with the nation's first private grant-making organization, the Fundación Venezolana contra la Parálisis Infantil in 1942. Nine years later he created the Eugenio Mendoza Foundation with a gift of nearly $1.5 million, the income of which was spent for agriculture, child-care programs, and the humanities. Mendoza and his foundation were also prime movers in the creation of the Asociación Dividendo Voluntario para la Comunidad (1964), a group of corporate donors who annually pledge up to 5 percent of their company's earnings for social, educational, and community betterment schemes, and of the Second International Conference of Foundations and Business Leaders held in Caracas in 1981. For a more detailed account of some of his activities, see Nathaniel Spear III, "Venezuela's Philanthropic Climate," *Foundation News* 13, no. 6 (November–December 1972): 31–34.

4. Indian foundation development is a particularly interesting phenomenon. The efforts of the Tata family are a case in point. Like the Rockefellers in America, the Tatas established a string of major foundations over a series of generations. Their efforts began in 1892, when J. N. Tata first sent promising Indian students to England for administrative and technical training. By 1938, when the Jamestji Nusserwanji Tata Endowment for the Higher Education of Indians was formally incorporated, hundreds of students had received travel grants for study in the arts, sciences, medicine, engineering, and civil services. Sir Ratan Tata funded a number of archaeological projects and nationalistic efforts at the turn of the century, including the work of the young Gandhi. J. R. D. and M. K. Tata established other trusts in 1944 and 1958. One of the most active members, Sir Dorabji Tata, founded the Lady Meherbai D. Tata Memorial Trust (1932, for blood-disease research), the Institute of Social Sciences (1936), the Tata Institute of Fundamental Research (1945, for nuclear research), and the Sir Dorabji Tata Trust (1941).

5. Despite the fact that business giving has traditionally hovered around the 1 percent mark, Congress recently raised the ceiling on corporate giving to 10 percent. U.S. corporate largesse has continued to expand since the 1950s, surpassing giving by the nation's private foundations for the first time in 1979.

6. The Creole Foundation was created by Venezuela's leading oil producer, the Creole Petroleum Corporation, for the support of educational, scientific, cultural, and social welfare concerns. Fundación Shell

was active primarily in agricultural programs. These foundations joined with Eugenio Mendoza in the creation of the Asociación Dividendo Voluntario para la Comunidad, a group of Venezuelan corporate donors.

7. A collaborative venture from the outset, the project has received substantial financial and advisory aid from the Ford Foundation and a variety of other U.S. grant makers. Its activities currently include a range of foreign and domestic research projects and study missions, conferences, and symposia for Japanese, U.S., and European foundation leaders. By 1979 a new emphasis on internationalizing Japanese philanthropy had begun to emerge. Efforts are currently under way to marshal Japanese business support for a variety of philanthropic undertakings in Southeast Asia.

8. Two of the most provocative sources on recent developments in Japanese philanthropy are Datus C. Smith, "Japanese Private Philanthropy," *Foundation News* 21, no. 3 (May–June 1980): 29–32; and an article by the head of the Japanese Center for International Exchange, Tadashi Yamamoto, entitled "Philanthropy in Japan: Memorandum from Tokyo," *Foundation News* 16, no. 1 (February 1975): 36–39. As Yamamoto explains, many of these foundations were initiated "in direct response to the mounting charges against corporations, and in the hope of fulfilling their 'social responsibility' " (p. 37).

9. Unlike its U.S. counterparts, the Asian Community Trust is almost exclusively international in scope, providing development funds for education, scientific research, medical and health care, social welfare, youth activities, and environmental protection throughout Southeast Asia. Initiated with the aid of the JCIE and managed by eight of Japan's leading banks, the trust collects and disseminates information on promising programs and works to promote private assistance throughout Southeast Asia.

The Fondation de France is more domestically oriented. Only about 250 private foundations are currently in operation in France, and their holdings are exceedingly modest. And yet there are those who maintain that private initiative has a meaningful role to play in French society, for, as one source explains, the state "is not permitted to finance innovative social or scientific research projects which have not yet proven their utility." The creation of the Fondation de France in 1969 was an important step in this direction. Based directly on U.S. community trusts, the foundation was developed through the combined initiative of the nation's fifteen largest banks. It operates nationwide and is empowered to receive funds and in-kind donations for causes of the donor's choice. Gifts can also be used to set up individual foundations under its management. Several priority areas have been designated for donors of small sums, including aid to the handicapped, the aged, troubled children, scientific research, urban planning, cultural activities, and programs in the Third World. The foundation has embarked on a concerted campaign to popularize the foundation ideal in France and to keep the public apprised of new funding opportunities. Several successful drives have been initiated under its sponsorship, including the Crusade of Hearts to aid mentally handicapped children (1970) and a 1975 campaign to alleviate the Solitude of the Aged, which raised $6 million and $2.5 million, respectively.

By the end of its first decade, the Fondation de France had received nearly forty-five thousand donations of $2,000–$5,000 each and had expanded its operations to include offices in Paris, Lyon, Marseille, and Angers. Fondation de France, *1969–1979* (Paris: Fondation de France, n.d.), p. 8.

10. Founded to commemorate the three-hundredth anniversary of the Bank of Sweden, the oldest central bank in the world (which is owned by the Swedish Parliament), the Tercentenary Foundation is dedicated to the support of scientific research (including the humanities) related to Swedish concerns, particularly research on the effects of technical, economic, and social changes on society and individual citizens.

The Japan Foundation is markedly international and humanistic in focus. Included among its programs are artistic and scholarly exchanges, publication and distribution of books and periodicals of Japan, language training, and support of Japanese studies at foreign universities. The foundation's bases in Asia, North and South America, and Europe serve as worldwide clearinghouses for information and materials on Japanese studies. For a more detailed discussion of its activities, see the Japan Foundation, *Annual Report*, 1980–81, which is available in English.

11. Although the British government has always been friendly to the concept of charity, it has moved slowly in providing the necessary tax incentives to inspire individual largesse on a wide scale. The *Inland* v. *Pemsil* case upheld the tax-exempt status of charitable assets in 1891, but no comparable tax incentives for individual donors have been forthcoming. Nevertheless, the government has continued to display a vivid interest in maintaining the voluntary sector, despite the increasing comprehensiveness of public programs. Passage of the National Health Service Act in 1946 first brought the continued viability of the third sector into question, generating lively debates over whether the government should appropriate charitable endowments of private organizations. This controversy in turn led to the Nathan Committee inquiry into the role of English nonprofit organizations in the 1950s. The committee's findings reaffirmed the need for private initiative and encouraged third-sector agencies to assume a pioneering role as government services expanded. Rooted in the Reformation and molded by the imperatives of the welfare state, British philanthropy was to complement, rather than compete with, public initiative.

The Charities Act of 1960 elaborated upon these findings, mandating the registration of British charities, encouraging greater coordination between private agencies and local public services, and providing legal mechanisms for updating outmoded charitable charters to meet modern ends. In the process, the British government reaffirmed its commitment to the private voluntary spirit. Foundations as well as charitable organizations have benefited from this continuing encouragement, which has given rise to a score of internationally recognized leaders of the caliber of the Leverhulme Trust (1925) and the British branch of the Gulbenkian Foundation. Leverhulme, which was founded by the bequest of the first Viscount Leverhulme and endowed with shares of Unilever Limited (originally Lever Brothers), currently funds educational and research institutions, individual researchers, and academic interchange. For more information on Leverhulme and the Gulbenkian Foundation, see *Grants by the Leverhulme Trust: Policies and Procedures* (London: Leverhulme Trust, July 1981); *Grants by the Leverhulme Trust in 1980* (London: Leverhulme Trust, 1980); and the annual reports of the Gulbenkian U.K. branch.

12. Two examples of these new organizations are the Development Foundation of Turkey (1969), which is engaged in rural agricultural reform, and the Turkish Education Foundation (1967), which supports scholarships, student facilities, and research. Others provide nursing training and underwrite environmental research. For a more detailed account of Turkish developments, see Engin Ural, *Foundations in Turkey* (Ankara: Development Fund of Turkey, 1978).

13. For an excellent overview of European charitable tax laws, see Mary Mauksch, *Corporate Voluntary Contributions in Europe* (New York: The Conference Board, 1982).

14. *Foundations Today: Current Facts and Figures on Private Foundations* (New York: The Foundation Center, 1980), p. 6.

15. Founded in 1972 by representatives of a variety of Latin American foundations, SOLIDARIOS coordinates jointly funded programs, administers private development funds, and serves as a clearinghouse for Latin America's third sector.

16. *Guide to European Foundations;* H. V. Hodson, ed., *The International Foundation Directory* (London: Europa Publications, 1979), passim.

17. Myer Foundation, *Annual Report,* 1980, p. 3. According to Meriel Wilmot, who was then the executive secretary of the Myer Foundation, "Of the major foundations set up in Australia in the past ten years none fund the humanities—they are principally welfare-oriented, with a few having strong interests in the arts." Meriel Wilmot to Kathleen D. McCarthy, July 7, 1981.

18. *Italy: A Country Shaped by Man* (Turin: Fondazione Giovanni Agnelli, 1981).

19. Founded in 1959 to promote humanities and scientific research in universities and research institutes, particularly in Germany, the Thyssen Foundation was created by the widow of one of Germany's richest industrialists, who had made his fortune in steel. In 1960 the foundation's assets were valued at approximately 100 million DM, much of the interest of which was subsequently allocated for the study of international relations, education, the arts, and the humanities.

20. Myer Foundation, *Annual Report,* 1981, p. 1.

21. Nuffield Foundation, *Annual Report,* 1978–79, quoted in Myer Foundation, *Annual Report,* 1981, p. 2.

22. Gulbenkian Foundation, U.K. and Commonwealth Branch, *Annual Report,* 1981, p. 3.

7 / British Foundations and the Humanities

RONALD C. TRESS

This article is the first of three case studies of foreign foundation activities. As Ronald C. Tress points out, few English foundations engage in international grant making, and fewer still fund the humanities. A second important point, which is echoed in Otto Häfner's essay on the German situation, is the dilemma of the "pioneers and pensioners": new pressures in the face of governmental cutbacks which threaten to cast foundations in a less innovative role. The issues which Tress raises are applicable to many other European, U.S., and Australian foundations as well, a fact that underscores the increasingly international nature of foundation concerns.

CHARITIES, TRUSTS, AND FOUNDATIONS

The philosopher Ludwig Wittgenstein, in the final paragraph of his *Tractatus Logico-Philosophicus,* wrote: "Whereof one cannot speak, thereof one must be silent."[1] I was tempted to quote the finality of this dictum when asked to provide an essay on British foundation support for the humanities, for the truth is that, while quite a bit may be said about the past, there is little by way of present trends to record. The first thing to be said, whether of past, present, or future, is that British foundations as such do not formally exist. They constitute an ill-defined genus of a much larger—though still ill-defined—species: the British charity. The origins of the charity lie in the Middle Ages when the rich gave to the poor as a Christian duty, and a bequest of property at death for purposes beneficial to the community was reckoned a prudent purchase of relief from the threatened sufferings of Purgatory.

The post-Reformation law of Elizabeth I, the Statute of Charitable Uses, passed in 1601, the same year as the first Poor Law directing local parishes to levy a rate on property for the relief of poverty, carried over those medieval sentiments. Charitable purposes were given in the statute's preamble as

the relief of aged, impotent and poor people; the maintenance
of sick and maimed soldiers and mariners, schools of learning,
free schools and scholars in universities; the repair of bridges,
ports, havens, causeways, churches, sea-banks and highways;
the education and preferment of orphans; the relief, stock or
maintenance for houses of correction; the marriage of poor
maids; the supportation, aid and help of young tradesmen,
handicraftsmen and persons decayed; the relief or redemption
of prisoners or captives; and the aid of ease of any poor inhab-
itants concerning payment of fifteens, setting out of soldiers
and other taxes.

The list has one odd inclusion—the repair of bridges, ports, and
highways—and one surprising exclusion—apart from the repair
of churches, there is no mention of religion. Otherwise, the
preamble is to this day the basis of British charity law, to be
applied by the same body as was then established for the purpose,
the Charity Commissioners. It is one of the conventions of Britain's famous unwritten constitution that governments and parlia-
ments do not legislate to define "charity" but leave the definition
to the courts and the Charity Commissioners. As recently as
1981, the minister responsible in Mrs. Thatcher's government
stated:

> While the criteria for this purpose may be imprecise, there was
> value in such imprecision which enabled case law to develop in
> accordance with contemporary needs. The Charity Commis-
> sion was constantly reassessing its own criteria—for example,
> in developing principles for deciding the charitable status of
> organisations now being set up to help the unemployed. A
> measure of how difficult it would be to redefine charitable
> status was that no-one had produced a new definition which
> was in any way an improvement upon the present one.[2]

Of course, as the minister implied, the law governing English
charities has not stood frozen since 1601. Case law made by
judges and interpretations by the Charity Commissioners have
altered its boundaries with the times. But the central area has
stood unchanged, and it is within that area that the vast majority
of English charities still lie: small-scale rights in properties or
funds yielding a modest income for local benefit. In England,
Wales, and Scotland there are some 115,000 such. Furthermore,

British income tax law has stuck to the same criteria. In contrast to the situation in the United States, there is no recognition in the British income tax of "foundations." The most one has is a declaration in 1891 by the House of Lords as the final court of appeal that income tax relief is due to all charities, in a fourfold classification: (1) the relief of poverty; (2) the advancement of education; (3) the advancement of religion; and (4) "other purposes beneficial to the community"—a description that leaves the debate wide open.

Hence, while in Britain we have of late come to accept the U.S. usage of *foundation* as the generic term for a permanent institution *founded* by a founder through the bestowal of a large donation of property (most often in the form of a stockholding in private enterprise), the income from which is to be used for prescribed philanthropic—or, as we should say, charitable—purposes, the word *foundation* is far from universal. The first such foundation in Britain was the Carnegie United Kingdom Trust, founded by Andrew Carnegie in 1913 with a block of his stockholding in the United States Steel Corporation transmitted from the United States to his native Scotland. Other trusts followed: the Barrow and Geraldine S. Cadbury Trust in 1921; the Leverhulme Trust in 1925; the Pilgrim Trust in 1930; the Joseph Rowntree Memorial Trust, in its present-day form, in 1959. Some more recent creations have taken the title of foundation, the Nuffield Foundation in 1943 and the Wolfson Foundation in 1955 being the most prominent. But the oldest foundation of all in name, the City Parochial Foundation, was created by an 1883 Act of Parliament which parceled up numerous old charitable properties attached to the City of London's many churches. And to confuse matters finally, Britain's largest foundation dedicated to medical and veterinary research is the Wellcome Trust; the Wellcome Foundation is the commercial pharmaceutical enterprise from which the Wellcome Trust, as sole shareholder, derives its income.

In all this welter of charities, trusts, and foundations, how fare the humanities? The answer is that, at best, they are a minority interest; for most, they are of no interest at all. The 1981 *Directory of Grant-Making Trusts*—a directory for grant seekers which lists all the known grant-making charitable bodies with an income of not less than £1,000—has a classification by objects under nine heads which extends to 377 pages (most bodies appearing under more than one head).[3] Of those 377 pages, names of charities giving grants for welfare occupy 118; those for medicine and health occupy 81; those for education, 37; and those for religion, 34. The arts and humanities grouped together get 19 pages, and the majority of entries are for the arts: painting and sculpture, dance, music and opera, drama, and film and television, with their physical accompaniments of art galleries and theaters. The rest of the humanities grants are mostly for the funding of libraries and museums.

CARNEGIE AND LIBRARIES

Libraries are the entry point of the modern foundation into British social history. The Carnegie United Kingdom Trust was the last of the foundations established by Andrew Carnegie and did not match in scale the Carnegie Corporation of New York, which he had established two years earlier, in 1911. But, for Britain, the trust was remarkable not only for its size but for its terms of reference and for the way they were interpreted. The trust deed reads: ". . . for the improvement of the well-being of the masses of the people of Great Britain and Ireland, by such means as are embraced within the meaning of the word 'charitable' according to Scotch or English Law, and which the Trustees might from time to time select as best fitted from age to age for securing these purposes, remembering that new needs are constantly arising as the masses advance." As to interpretation, the terms might have been taken as one more contribution to the relief of poverty and disease. But that was not the intention of either Carnegie or his trustees. Carnegie himself laid emphasis on libraries and music. The latter was, shall we say, somewhat narrowly conceived, since it took the single-minded form of the restoration of church organs. Carnegie's conception for libraries, on the other hand, was grand-scale.

A Public Libraries Act enabling local authorities to build libraries and furnish them with books had been on the statute book since 1850, but few authorities had taken advantage of its powers. It was Andrew Carnegie, first personally and then through the Carnegie United Kingdom Trust, who got the action going. Before 1913 and the establishment of the trust he had helped to finance almost three hundred municipal libraries in the

United Kingdom, more than half of the total in existence. By the time of the foundation, the leaven had begun to work. Municipal authorities were not only building libraries but filling them with books, and the trust was able to shift its attention from the towns to the rural areas, from municipal libraries to county library services. Then, when enabling legislation caught up with this new initiative, the trust moved on again: to the professional training of librarians and, the crowning achievement, a central library service with a chain of communications which made a complete lending service available to all serious scholars, wherever in the British Isles they were located and whatever the subject.

The Carnegie United Kingdom Trust's role in the development of British library services is worth recalling merely as an outstanding example in the catalog of contributions by British foundations to the humanities. The trust's innovations, however, had a more general significance. First, they marked a major departure from the traditional charitable concerns toward a concern for the quality of life, for the arts and humanities. As one of the trustees observed when reviewing in 1963 the trust's first fifty years, while the trust had made contributions to the solutions of the social problems of unemployment and malnutrition, handicap and disability, "by far the greater part of the Trust's concern has been to encourage the devising and development of those instruments and activities which aimed to raise the level of the pursuits, the interests and the enjoyments of the generality of our people." Second, they represented an attitude toward the statutory and voluntary sectors of provision and toward the public and private domains of national life. Here also I quote the jubilee celebrant:

> The essential work of the Trust has been to do two things: to pioneer in a few areas of what is now public and statutory action, and perhaps even more important, to help to release and to support the efforts of groups of citizens, of all faiths and of none . . . who have sought by their own free service to improve the conditions and the opportunities of their fellows.[4]

From here on, I shall dwell upon this text.

PIONEERS AND PENSIONERS

The phrase "to pioneer . . . what is now public and statutory action" is a fair description of a large part of the activity of British foundations over the last sixty-odd years. Most patently this is the case in what have been, and continue to be, the two most intensive areas of charitable activity: the relief of poverty and disease and the advancement of education. The statutory social services of Britain were all pioneered by charities and charitable foundations, some directly, others through voluntary efforts with charitable fund support. In education, the Leverhulme Trust, like many others on a smaller scale before it, was established to provide "scholarships for research and education" and has had to widen its interpretation of scholarships to embrace research and teaching fellowships, studentships, and the like, as school and university education has become increasingly, in all countries, a matter of state and public authority provision.

But, while the pioneering role of the foundations is still open to new ideas and initiatives, a new concern has of late arisen: a recognition that the well-trodden route from private and privately funded initiative to nationwide public service is not the best for every kind of traffic, that some lines best remain the subject of private voluntary endeavor. This experience is so far most powerful among the social services. We have lately come to acknowledge that there are areas of social work where the fact that a service is official and manned by professionals is in itself a barrier to its use by those who are most in need; where, therefore, the voluntary organizations have not just an initial pioneering task but a permanent, complementary role. And with this discovery, there come new problems: First, for the service itself, there is acknowledgment that while the trained professional may be unwelcome, the untrained amateur can be dangerous; second, for the supportive charities and foundations, if voluntary organizations become their long-term dependents, funds are no longer free for fresh ventures.

To date, in the arts and humanities, the same kind of nodal point has not been reached. There is plenty of pioneering to be done which may, it is hoped, lead on to broader state provision. The municipal libraries and museums, rural library services, and central library services have now all become large-scale activities and the responsibility of central and local government. In fine art and music, the biggest single provider by far today is the Arts Council of Great Britain, a body financed entirely by central government. The promotional endeavors of the foundations have therefore moved in substantial measure to supporting amateur participation in the arts or the new phenomenon, community arts. The Carnegie United Kingdom Trust, for example, runs a special scheme to aid what it regards as underdeveloped arts, such as mime and puppetry, and national schemes designed to improve amateur standards, as with music and drama festivals, and in particular to pioneer the arts for, and by, the disabled.

The Calouste Gulbenkian Foundation, founded in 1956, is of Portuguese nationality, but almost from the outset it has had a separate branch in London to serve Britain and the Commonwealth. The activities of the branch in the Commonwealth have been modest and have concentrated upon education and race relations. In Britain, however, the arts have been accorded more than half its disbursements, and besides its own funding activities, the reports it has commissioned—*Help for the Arts* in 1959, *Support for the Arts in England and Wales* in 1976—have greatly influenced both other foundations and government.

When Gulbenkian began in Britain, the Arts Council was in its infancy, with most of its limited funds going to support professional opera and ballet in London. Gulbenkian set about promoting regional arts associations and building theaters on provincial university campuses to provide cultural growth points—a policy backed by Nuffield, Wolfson, Rayne, and other foundations—as well as providing support for arts centers, exhibitions, study grants, traveling scholarships, artists in residence, and so on. Increasingly over the last decade, however, Gulbenkian and some other foundations have sought to relate their support for the arts and creative artists to their social concerns. In Gulbenkian's case, there is now, first, a program of "Arts for All," promoting every kind of means of involving creative artists in everyday life and making their work accessible to people who do not usually experience the arts; and second, the development of community arts, with self-help groups in deprived areas as a main social welfare priority.

Looking ahead in this direction, however, I see in prospect some of the very problems I have noted as existing in the welfare field. One cannot envisage the government-financed Arts Council being so ready to take over this class of activity, the pioneering done, as it has been to support the professional arts or regional arts associations. Nor can one imagine such an official body being welcome. But will the pioneering foundations accept that they have acquired near-permanent commitments?

When we turn to the humanities other than the arts—philosophy, history, archaeology, ancient and modern languages and literatures—we almost inevitably move out of the world of the general public, of everyday life in communities, into the world of scholarship and learning centered on the universities. Since British universities are largely state funded, with fees and annual block grants calculated to allow academic staff time for research, with clerical support and library facilities, it was long assumed that the humanities generally were implicitly provided for. It was only after a report in 1961, initiated by the Pilgrim Trust, sponsored by the British Academy, and financed by the Rockefeller Foundation, that the need for specific financial support for research in the humanities was acknowledged by the British government and an annual grant of public funds instituted, to be administered—since there was and is no Research Council coverage for the humanities—by the British Academy, the self-selecting body of the humanities' elite.

In contrast to the case of the Arts Council, however, the government's grant to the British Academy has not grown from such small beginnings to dominant patronage. It has remained small, leaving the funding role of the foundations interested in humanities unchanged. The Pilgrim Trust, to which reference has been made, was founded in 1930 by an American, Edward Harkness, but as a British institution designed for the benefit of Britain. Like so many of its kind, it concentrated in its early activities on social welfare. After World War II, however, the trust's attention was extended to the promotion of the arts and learning and preservation of the national heritage, particularly of churches and other historic buildings. The trust's support for learning is mostly in the form of capital grants, occasionally substantial but more often on a modest scale.

The Leverhulme Trust was founded in 1925 by the creator of Lever Brothers, now part of the Unilever multinational enterprise, and in accordance with his will, grants are invariably for expenditure on people: research and teaching fellowships, studentships, and the like. Though it is constrained in its type of funding, there are no constraints on the subjects eligible for its support, and the trust's grants range through all disciplines. Over the past decade, the subjects within the humanities which have received most research support have been archaeology, British and foreign history, and English language and literature; scholarship awards have centered on young musicians.

The most that has been done in the way of policy, however, has been, first, a readiness to consider applications from this quarter and, second, an insistence upon quality and innovation as the bases of selection. Only thus may one explain a research-grant list which embraces the preservation of ancient Jewish literature and of organic materials brought up from a sunken Tudor battleship; environmental archaeology at York, in the Cusichaca valley of Peru, and at Viking settlements around the North Atlantic; a maritime history of the Channel Islands; an edition of the writings of Peter Abelard; research for a museum of the romantic poets of the English Lake District; a directory of African languages and survey of African orthographies; and a study of the religious experience of the Tibetan peoples of the Himalayas. A more definite policy has operated in the funding of schemes for the interchange of scholars and students between the United Kingdom and other countries, among Commonwealth countries, and between Commonwealth and foreign countries. But these have been open at least as much to scientists as to humanists.

Research funding in the humanities presents few of the pioneering and development problems noted elsewhere. Archaeological excavations can be endless, and some literary and historical studies can take on that appearance if allowed to do so. Even in these cases, however, the research can be parceled up into manageable stages. Elsewhere, research typically comprises finite projects of modest (three to five years') duration.

Support for educational innovation is a different matter. Besides the massive advances in provision for schools already referred to, the experience of universities and other institutions of higher and further education in the thirty years which followed World War II was one of steady expansion in which, therefore, curricular and teaching innovations could be funded by foundations with the confident assurance that, if successful, they would be incorporated into the normal, state-funded system. An end to educational expansion, now followed by financial cutbacks, has destroyed this convenient assumption. For some while to come, universities and similar institutions will be grappling with matters of frozen posts and staff redundancies. Subject rationalization even on the crudest terms will take time. Ahead, however, one must begin to look for ways of combining academic innovation in subjects and in methods with conditions of zero growth. It may require from the foundations a new style of pioneering.

THE THIRD WORLD

What then of British foundations and the humanities in the context of the Third World? Implicit in the preamble to the Elizabethan Statute of Charitable Uses which I quoted at the beginning of this essay is the oft-quoted English adage that charity begins at home. The bulk of the activity of the British foundations is directed at the United Kingdom. Even where this exclusiveness is not, as it is so often, obligatory by the terms of the foundation's trust deed, it tends nevertheless to apply in practice. The foundations whose titles allow them to support activities outside the British Isles—more often extending to the Commonwealth only, rather than to the world at large—in fact apply only a very limited proportion of their funds to activities in these areas, and that portion mostly to health and welfare ventures. The London branch of the Calouste Gulbenkian Foundation includes the Commonwealth in its terms; the Leverhulme Trust tends to favor the Commonwealth, although it suffers no geographical constraint. In both cases, however, in the kinds of activity chosen to benefit from their funding, the foundations display no evident policy other than to support what comes their way if it shows originality and imagination and promises to contribute to well-being, knowledge, or cultural life in the country concerned.

The fact is that the British institutions with a commitment to the arts and humanities are few, and those with horizons beyond Britain's shores are fewer. Furthermore, their funds are limited. The days when one foundation could materially affect a problem, as Carnegie did for libraries in Britain, have long since ceased. The foundations can still pioneer, but on the scale of experiment only. The scale of development which needs to follow successful experiment must find its finance elsewhere.

NOTES

1. Ludwig Wittgenstein, *Tractatus Logico-Philosophicus* (London: Routledge and Kegan Paul, 1962), p. 243.

2. Timothy Raison, M.P., Minister of State, Home Office, Speech before Northampton Council of Voluntary Service, 1981.

3. *Directory of Grant-Making Trusts* (Kent: Charities Aid Foundation, 1981).

4. Sir Hector Hetherington, Speech delivered in Dunfermline, Scotland, October 3, 1963, quoted in William Robertson, *Welfare in Trust: A History of the Carnegie United Kingdom Trust, 1913–1963* (Dunfermline: The Carnegie United Kingdom Trust, 1964), p. 261.

8 / Foundations and Government Support for the Humanities in Germany

OTTO HÄFNER

Like the preceding essay, this one explores the changing relationships between public and private funding in a European setting. As director of the social sciences division of one of Europe's largest foundations, Otto Häfner has participated in many of the developments he describes. As he explains, even the most well-endowed private funders can only supplement, rather than supplant, governmental efforts, so that public and private cooperation is a vital element in the continuation of many of Germany's most important humanistic ventures.

I

When talking about the relationship between foundation and government sponsorship of the humanities in the Federal Republic of Germany, it is important to remember that in Germany *philanthropy* is still a rarely used foreign word. Responsibility for public welfare, which includes the support of the natural, social, and humanistic sciences, has traditionally been considered one of the government's tasks and privileges. This tendency has had a lasting influence. In comparison with the traditionally dominant role of government, private sources have relatively little financial power. These organizations have also experienced a considerable loss of their financial substance as a result of two world wars and subsequent monetary reform. Moreover, foundations modeled on the example of large U.S. philanthropic foundations were established in Germany only after 1945, and unlike U.S. foundations, the most important of these were bound to the specific, restricted purpose of promoting sciences. The Volkswagen and the Fritz Thyssen foundations exemplify this trend. The government also establishes and finances foundations, such as the Stiftung Preussischer Kulturbesitz in Berlin, which have a significant impact on cultural policy. As a result, private foundations play only a supplementary, although a stimulating and important, role in the promotion of cultural and scientific activities in West Germany.

II

The eleven German states (Länder) have the most important role in the domain of university research and teaching. The Länder are responsible for the universities, for which they spend about 17 billion DM ($7.4 billion) annually. No university or part of a university is financed by private sources. The federal government promotes research and development through two ministries and various departments outside the universities and gives money mainly for major research projects. These activities consume another 12 billion DM. Thus, public expenses for science, technology, social sciences, and humanistic studies amounted to 29 billion DM in 1980. According to estimates, private business and industry spend another 17 billion DM for research and development annually, so that a total amount of 46 billion DM ($20 billion) is spent for these purposes in the Federal Republic.

This should be seen as the background against which one has to consider the figures for private foundations, which spend between 200 and 250 million DM annually for the support of scientific research, the largest amount of which was given (in 1979) by the Volkswagen Foundation (114 million DM), the Stifterverband für die Deutsche Wissenschaft (22 million DM), and the Fritz Thyssen Foundation (7.7 million DM). Considering these figures, one might gain the impression that private foundations hardly influence the funding of scientific research. Examples prove, however, that they are of considerable importance for the development of new fields of research and research institutions. They are particularly significant for humanistic studies, on which private foundations spend a decisive amount of their means (Volkswagen, 39.9 percent; Thyssen, 46.8 percent). They are even more necessary and important because the federal government does not have its own programs in the humanities, as it does in the natural sciences and technology.

As a result, foundation funding, if spent as intelligently as possible, can play an important role. Foundation grants can be used as starting aids or for matching; they can be used for specific programs, such as the postgraduate programs of the sixties or the revitalization of historical research undertaken some years ago; they can even offer a second chance in a system of research support which basically is characterized by public financing. Thus support for the humanities is not only important but a worthwhile endeavor which requires initiative, ideas, and the readiness to take risks.

III

This financial and organizational system is a politically sensitive and rather complicated network. Some people consider it inefficient, while others believe that it provides a form of protection against central regulation and offers an opportunity for variety in the cultural and scientific arena where it is most urgently needed.

Foundations must have a fairly good knowledge of this system if they wish to support the humanities, especially if their support is long-term. Let me illustrate this claim by an example. The central government and the eleven Länder agreed to support jointly a number of major research institutes, projects, and particularly important research organizations (e.g., the Max-Planck-Society [MPG] and the German Research Society [DFG]).[1] After long and difficult negotiations they finally in 1975 reached a skeleton agreement for the support of research which provided governmental financing for projects of particular scientific and cultural significance. This agreement has been important for the Volkswagen Foundation. The completion of several music editions (e.g., Bach, Haydn, Gluck, Mozart, Schubert, and Schoenberg) for which the foundation has spent a considerable amount of money (more than 7 million DM over a number of years) and which were uncertain for a long time has now been guaranteed. Many other long-term projects, such as dictionaries or editions in theology, philosophy, history, or archaeology, have been included in the financing. Some of these, including the research activities of the two greatest German museums, have been in progress for decades and may not be completed before the end of the first quarter of the next century. Thus, private funders of research, particularly in the humanities and cultural activities, cannot afford to overlook the possibilities and limits of long-term government sponsorship. At a time when public finances are restricted it is particularly important to look for new ideas and sources of support for the humanities.

IV

One of the key issues of this conference concerns the roles and priorities which will shape efforts to develop humanities programs in the 1980s and the ways in which the balance of responsibility will be distributed among governments, private foundations, and multinational corporations. Before I enter into specifics on the background of the Volkswagen Foundation's funding activities, I would like to mention a discussion on the future of the humanities which was supported by the foundation in mid-1981. A number of leading experts from the United States, various European countries, and the Federal Republic of Germany took part in this discussion, among them Saul Bellow, Edward Shils, and Karl Weintraub from the University of Chicago; Gordon Ray of the Guggenheim Foundation; John Passmore from Canberra; and Walter Ruegg from Switzerland. Professor Rudolf Vierhaus, a German historian, and Professor Bernhard Fabian, a German anglicist, were the organizers. There had already been a preliminary conference in 1978, reported in *Minerva*.[2]

What was the experts' diagnosis? The discussion began with the observation that within both the academic world and the larger cultural context the humanities no longer have the unchallenged position which they held in the past and continued to hold until even a few decades ago. It became clear that the present state of the humanities is a new situation which is marked by a number of paradoxes:

- The humanities as academic disciplines seem to be in a state of relative decline, while at the same time large-scale cultural needs which can only be satisfied by the humanities are being expressed.
- It is too early to say whether the humanities will follow "big science" in its exodus from the universities, but (with a view to international developments) an increasing proportion of scientific research is now being carried on outside universities; and the transformation from research centers or research-centered institutions to predominantly educational institutions continues.
- On the other hand, there seems to be a growing awareness of the dangers that might attend the retreat of the humanities

into privacy and security. The participants agreed upon the necessity of an in-depth consideration of problems in various areas of humanistic research. For example, large-scale projects such as editions and dictionaries call for a new type of research establishment. Likewise, the increasingly large reservoirs of literature necessary for individual research in special research libraries necessitate the development of new techniques to cope with the floods of literature now inundating practically every field of humanistic scholarship. New forms and opportunities for international collaboration should be created. With the general decline in the knowledge of foreign languages, new media for international communication have to be devised. The role which translations of scholarly works will play in the future also has to be determined. Finally, practical interdisciplinary work ought to result in a closer interaction between the humanities and the social sciences.

These problems were discussed over the course of the three-day meeting. Of course, other issues were raised as well. For example, the question what the humanities can offer to enhance future cultural and political developments in Western democracies was explored. What can the humanities contribute from their experience? How can they leave their defensive role? Have they learned to interact with other disciplines? Are the humanities too oriented toward what is politically feasible and financially realizable? A reorganization of the disciplinary system to cope with the increasing numbers of special disciplines, academic teachers, printed matter, and expenses was judged strictly essential.

Of course, many more questions were asked than could be answered. But there is still one more comment which is worth repeating: The present uncertainty about and in the humanities is not so much an organizational or a financial question as an intellectual one, and the answer will be decisive in determining how the humanities will relate to new worldwide developments.

V

Let us return to the question of support. Gordon N. Ray gave a lecture during the 1981 conference entitled "The Climate of Support for the Humanities," in which he described the indifference of the American public toward humanistic studies, stating that "nobody is against them (except when their supporters are confused with secular humanists in hot pursuit of organized religion), but no considerable proportion of the population is strongly for them."[3]

It seems to me that the situation is similar in Germany, even though the importance of the humanities for the intellectual climate of the country and its cultural self-image is undoubted. But although the natural and engineering sciences and even part of the (applied) social sciences have been successful in raising money from official and private funding authorities, for various reasons the humanities have had more problems. One has of course to differentiate: Historians, for example, seem to be particularly successful in developing funding programs and raising money. In any case, during recent years history has experienced a definite renaissance. But there are a number of other disciplines which obviously have suffered from organizational changes within universities during the last decade. These are (in Germany at least) the classical disciplines such as art and music, ethnology, archaeology, classical philologies, and philosophy, all of which fare badly in foundation funding programs. This is the case with the Volkswagen Foundation, even though the proportion of its projects in the humanities is relatively large within the overall funding framework.

The difficulty is due, in part, to the fact that since the 1960s most of the private and official sponsors of research have increasingly preferred to set thematically defined priorities within their funding programs. The Volkswagen Foundation's funding program, which has five priorities (among twenty-seven) under which the foundation supports projects in the humanities, illustrates this development. History dominates three of the areas (Humanities, Science, and Technology: Historical Development and Social Context; Comparative European History and Historiography; Research on Cultural Heritage: Compilation, Classification, and Conservation). Humanists of various disciplines working in universities, archives, libraries, museums, and offices for the preservation of historical monuments may participate in these programs. A new initiative of the Volkswagen Foundation is the support of junior scholars in selected disciplines of the humanities, a matter to which I shall refer later.

There is no doubt that humanistic research is primarily individual research and that funding programs have to be strongly oriented toward this traditional working method. The German government does not provide substantial additional funds for research programs and research projects in the humanities. It is therefore not surprising that the majority of scholars financed since 1971 under the terms of the foundation's particularly successful program of Academy Scholarships have been humanists, especially historians and psychologists.

There are two other major projects funded by the foundation that I would like to mention in this context, the history of which serves to illustrate the special relationship between private and public funding in Germany. The Volkswagen Foundation provided start-up costs for the establishment of an Institute for Advanced Studies, the Wissenschaftskolleg zu Berlin, after several unsuccessful attempts to fund such a center in the 1960s. Plans for this new (and unique) institution in Germany were developed three years ago, following consultations with scholars and representatives from comparable institutions in the United States and Western Europe. The idea had always been welcomed, but problems such as location, the high cost of investment and follow-up financing, and lack of support from the political-administrative arena impeded its realization.

The idea of establishing such an institute—which would be open to all disciplines in the humanities, social sciences, and natural sciences and would offer the necessary conditions for individual and collective scientific work—was welcomed by the Land Berlin and its government from the outset. It was also important to gain the support of the major German scientific organizations and central governmental authorities, and this was done successfully. The institute was established one year ago, when the necessary buildings were purchased and renovated, and the first fifteen fellows from Germany, other European countries, and abroad will soon be in Berlin for one year. Incidentally, the first group of fellows consists primarily of humanists, a clear indication that the work which will be done in Berlin will include the humanities.

This new project, in which the Volkswagen Foundation has been intensively engaged, is of course meant to have a long-range effect. On the other hand, it would exceed the foundation's financial sources to raise all the necessary funding for the first ten years, the period which, as experience has shown, an institution needs for its organization and consolidation. Nor would other private sponsors in the Federal Republic be in a position to raise the funds required for the normal day-to-day work for several years.

For projects of this kind it is therefore a vital question right from the beginning whether—and when—the government will decide to secure long-term financing. The foundation was able to give only the decisive impulse and impetus. We hope that the Wissenschaftskolleg will become active and gain intellectual impact in the sense of the issues discussed at this conference.

The institute in Berlin is one example of how private and governmental funding organizations can combine their resources for a particularly interesting and difficult project. Another example illustrates how the foundation became active in response to diminishing governmental efforts (some people even call it failure) in a very important area. I am referring to an issue which has been widely discussed in Germany: the provision of support for junior scholars through scholarships for postgraduates. A declared objective of the federal government and the Länder governments, postgraduate support programs had been financed at 50–60 million DM annually since the beginning of the seventies. Apart from the fact that since the middle of the seventies funds were provided only in the form of loans, because of budgetary constraints, governmental activities in this field have always been rather controversial. However, one must not forget that private sources for postgraduate support are very limited. The Thyssen Foundation engaged in postgraduate support to a small extent in the early sixties, and Volkswagen to a larger extent later. But apart from awarding a few research fellowships, foundations withdrew from this area after the government became active.

By 1981 it had become obvious that there was no hope for continued governmental postgraduate support, and it was reported that within some humanistic disciplines it was becoming increasingly difficult to attract talented young people to do research, owing to limited career opportunities. With this situation in mind, the Volkswagen Foundation decided to launch a program for the promotion of junior scholars through the support of Ph.D. programs within selected disciplines in the humanities, including classical philology, philosophy, religion, arts, theater, music, ethnology, and archaeology. We hoped that such an initiative might have a trend-setting effect. The response thus far shows that such expectations were correct. The first of two application deadlines resulted in dozens of highly qualified applications.

Of course it would be neither possible nor very wise to consider foundations as a replacement for government support. The activity of the Volkswagen Foundation or any other private institution can address only the special requirements of specific disciplines and will always have to remain within the scope of its own financial means.

NOTES

1. The DFG is the central self-governing organization of science, the social sciences, and the humanities. In 1980 the DFG spent about 89 million DM, approximately 11 percent of its budget, for the humanities.

2. Bernhard Fabian and Rudolf Vierhaus, "The Calling and Condition of the Humanistic Disciplines—The Future of the Humanities: Report of a Conference," *Minerva* 17, no. 4 (Winter 1979): 549–54.

3. Unpublished conference paper, p. 7.

9 / An Overview of Japanese Philanthropy and International Cooperation in the Third World

KAZUE IWAMOTO

Kazue Iwamoto traces the historical roots of private foundation philanthropy in Japan, including the foundations' relationship with the Japanese government. After describing some of the legal constraints on funding for both the humanities and international undertakings, she explains her own program at Toyota, the "Know Our Neighbors" Translation-Publication Program, which is active throughout Southeast Asia, and then examines the role of such small, well-focused programs in the overall funding picture. Like Otto Häfner and Ronald C. Tress, Kazue Iwamoto has been an active participant in the programs she describes. It should also be noted that the Toyota Foundation pioneered in the training of professional program officers along American lines; Iwamoto is therefore one of her nation's first professional foundation program officers.

History shows that information flows from developed countries to developing countries. This flow of information is seldom reversed, whether in science and technology or in the humanities. Furthermore, although information on the West steadily flows into the East, data on their own neighboring countries are seldom available to Eastern countries. The situation is the same regarding information on the activities of foundations. Details on cooperation between the Third World and Japanese foundations are not available either in neighboring Eastern countries or in the West. Actually, such information is not well disseminated even inside Japan because of the short history of foundation activities there.

Japan's first philanthropic foundation, apart from philanthropy closely related to religion, was established on the basis of the accumulation of wealth in the Edo period (1603–1868), which represented the state of maturity in an agricultural society. In the history of Japan, the Edo period is very interesting: It marks the point at which the structure of the feudal system established with the birth of the Kamakura shogunate at the end of the twelfth century was perfected.

In the sixteenth century, Western ships began to visit Japan. Sensing the danger of colonization, the shogunate of the Edo period decided to deal only with Holland as a trade partner, and even the site of contact was restricted to a small island in southern Japan. The period of seclusion lasted two hundred years. During this time there were tremendous developments in Japanese culture, arts and sciences, and local industry, specifically in the social sciences, such as geography, economics, and legal study; in the natural sciences, such as astronomy, mathematics, surveying and measuring methods, pharmacology, and medicine; and in science and technology, including agricultural, mining, and industrial sciences.

In the humanities, *kokugaku* (or national studies, also known as *wagaku*, or Japanese studies, when contrasted with Chinese studies and Western studies) developed as a discipline between the middle of the seventeenth century and the middle of the nineteenth century. The ruling warrior class pursued Chinese studies, whereas *kokugaku* was widely studied not only by warriors but also by Shinto priests, physicians, Buddhist priests, merchants, and peasants. *Kokugaku* works included chiefly studies of Japanese history, classics produced by Japanese, thought, Shinto, and national structure (the concepts that characterize a nation, including its birth and the fundamental principles of its organization). The results of these studies became the basis of studies of Japanese literature, language, and history in the Meiji era (1868–1912). The works on Shinto and on national structure played a major role in the formation of thought in the Meiji era and later. During the Edo period, local culture flourished and a private sector developed. Education and science spread to provincial areas and among the common people. According to a study conducted by Dr. R. Dore, it is estimated that in 1868 43 percent of male children and 10 percent of female children attended school, at a time when the warrior class accounted for 6–7 percent of the population, the peasant class was more than 80 percent, and the merchant and other classes were 9 percent. Japan's first foundation was established by merchants at that time in order to assist starving children and the poor; however, it did not have a direct influence on later development of foundations in Japan.

About a century ago Japan opened its doors to the world, weathered the Meiji Restoration, established a constitutional government, and embarked upon the task of modernization. In order to resist the pressures of Western powers anxious to colonize Japan, it was necessary for the country to modernize and industrialize. For this purpose, with the leadership of a powerful central government, a high priority was placed on the development of science and technology. Even private foundations were not exempted from this policy. Under the capitalist economy that rapidly developed after the Sino-Japanese War (1894–95) and the Russo-Japanese War (1904–5), more than ten foundations, including Harada Sekizenkai, Saito Ho-onkai, Hattori Hokokai, and Mitsui Ho-onkai, were established in the space of about twenty years following 1915; however, these foundations were established on the initiative of the government or in order to share the burden of national policy. Thus, although these foundations seem to have contributed to the promotion of research in science and technology at that time, they are at present almost totally inactive because they were paralyzed by World War II and its consequent inflation.

Roughly one hundred years have passed since Japan began its modernization. Because modernization and industrialization were rapid and because Japan did not have the resources to devote attention to the impact of such rapid development, the social and natural environments have been skewed. Effective foundation activities should have been able to minimize such disturbances during the past hundred years, but for several reasons few foundations have yet been established: The accumulation of wealth that is the basis for the establishment of foundations has been insufficient; the concept of a third sector has not easily been formed, because development has had to be encouraged under a powerful centralized government; and foundations have had to follow the government's policy of placing a high priority on science and technology (even now endowment funds are tax exempt only when the foundation's activities are in science and technology). During the years of rapid development, foundations that placed a high priority on social sciences, humanities, and international cooperation were almost nonexistent. It was in the 1970s, a hundred years after the Meiji Restoration, that such institutions were first established.

As is clear from this brief history, Japanese foundations have almost no experience in international cooperation, especially in grant-making activities related to projects in the Third World. As a result, the grant-making activities of this sort initiated since the 1970s have all been experimental in nature. Since it has been natural for these experimental activities to choose the Third World region that is geographically closest, almost all such grants provided by present-day Japanese private foundations have been made in Southeast Asia. Thus the references to the Third World in the following discussion refer particularly to Southeast Asia.

Something should also be said about the size of Japanese private grant-making foundations. In 1978 Japan's total research and development expenditure was $17.6 billion; 72 percent of this figure was borne by the private, profit-making sector; 65 percent of this figure was expended in the industrial sector; 88 percent of this figure was expended on natural science and technology; and the rest was spent in the social sciences and humanities. Compared with these figures the grant budgets of private grant-making foundations were so close to zero as a percentage that it is difficult to understand the scope of foundation activities.

A comparison with the budget of the Ministry of Education's grant-in-aid for scientific research, which plays a major role in encouraging research activities in universities as well as research activities in the social sciences and humanities, is useful in this context. In 1980 the Ministry of Education's grants-in-aid for scientific research totaled $156 million, 7.6 percent of which amount was allocated to the humanities. Let us take the Toyota Foundation as an example of a private grant-making foundation: 1.25 percent of the Ministry of Education's grant-in-aid for scientific research is equivalent to the Toyota Foundation's total grant budget. Or compare the 1979 grant budget of the Ford Foundation, which is the largest U.S. private grant-making foundation: 2 percent of the Ford Foundation's grant budget is equivalent to the Toyota Foundation's total grant budget. The grant budgets of the semigovernmental Japan Foundation and Japan Society for the Promotion of Science, which are engaged in international exchange, are about the same, and each is equivalent to 12 percent of the Ford Foundation's grant budget. Even the total budget of the grant-in-aid for scientific research of the Ministry of Education is only 1.5 times more than the Ford Foundation's grant budget.

Japanese foundations making grants to international activities related to the Third World (including semigovernmental organizations and private grant-making foundations) are among those listed in Table 1. Among these foundations, organizations with endowments of more than $100 million are the Japan Shipbuilding Industry Foundation, the Japan Society for the Promotion of Science, and the Japan Foundation; organizations with endowments between $40 million and $70 million are the JEC Fund: Commemorative Association for the Japan World Exposition, 1970, the National Institute for Research Advancement, the Hoso Bunka Foundation, and the Toyota Foundation; organizations with endowments between $6 million and $15 million are the Iwatani Naoji Foundation, the Niwano Peace Foundation, and the Mitsubishi Bank Foundation; organizations with endowments between $1 million and $4 million are the Asahi Glass Company Scholarship Society, the Kajima Foundation, the Yoshida Foundation for Science and Technology, the Twenty-First Century Culture and Science Foundation, the Naito Foundation, the Matsumae International Foundation, the Kawakami Memorial Foundation, the Rotary Yoneyama Memorial Foundation, Inc., and the Tokyu Foundation for Inbound Students; and organizations with endowments below $1 million are the Imai Memorial Charitable Trust for Overseas Cooperation and the Asia Community Trust. However, the majority of these foundations make grants not only in the Third World but also in Japan and other parts of the world. The fields that they support include science and technology, Japanology, humanities, and social sciences, among others. I cannot report the ratio of the grant amounts awarded by these foundations in the Third World and in the humanities because I do not have such figures; however, it should not be difficult to imagine how small these figures are.

The impact of activities in international cooperation can be evaluated quantitatively and qualitatively, and both are important. The size of an organization engaged in such work determines what it can do and what it will find difficult to achieve; large organizations, for example, will not be very good at carrying out small programs with great care. In other words, there are different kinds of programs suitable for different sizes of organizations. If we overlooked this point, we would tend to make only quantitative comparisons and would fail to grasp the real situation.

When I visited the representative of a Western foundation in a

Table 1. MAJOR GRANT-MAKING FOUNDATIONS IN JAPAN
(NAME; YEAR OF ESTABLISHMENT; ENDOWMENT;
AND PRIMARY ACTIVITIES)

American Studies Foundation; 1962; $430,000; Promotes American studies through grants to universities, research institutions, groups, and individuals.

Asahi Children's Welfare Foundation; 1966; $2,170,000;* Provides financial assistance for programs that enhance the health and spirit of the nation's children and youth.

Asahi Glass Company Scholarship Society; 1957; $1,220,000; Provides scholarships to students in technical and nontechnical fields.

†Asahi Glass Industrial Technology Foundation; 1934; $6,520,000;* Provides aid for studies and research in industry and industrial technology.

‡‡Asia Community Trust; 1979; $202,869;* Provides grants for projects conducted in Asia in rural development, health, social welfare, education, and the environment.

C. Itoh Foundation; 1974; $5,520,000;* Conducts surveys and research on the problems of young people and provides aid to nonprofit activities that promote the development of young people.

Capital Markets Promotion Foundation; 1969; $178,260,000;* Provides financial assistance to programs for the protection of securities investments and to programs related to the growth of securities markets.

Chiyoda Mutual Life Foundation; 1966; $700,000; Disperses information on health care and disease prevention, provides grants for research and projects relating to disease prevention and other kinds of health-care activities, and conducts examinations and offers health consultation for people in local communities.

Daiwa Health Foundation; 1972; $570,000; Provides grants for survey research, disseminates information, and conducts surveys and research on the prevention of adult diseases.

Foundation for the Promotion of Research on Medicinal Resources; 1946; $1,830,000; Provides aid for basic and applied research that may lead to the discovery and development of new medicines.

Hakuho Foundation; 1970; $1,480,000; Awards prizes both to individuals and to organizations who have contributed to Japanese-language education at the primary school level and to the language education of children who have visual or auditory handicaps.

Table 1. *Continued*

Hatakeyama Cultural Foundation; 1960; $1,960,000; Provides financial assistance for research in science and technology, particularly in engineering and industrial technology.

Heart Memorial Foundation; 1972; $6,350,000;* Provides financial assistance for the improvement of facilities and equipment in elementary and junior high schools and for projects that improve social welfare, and provides grants for research on elementary and junior high school education and social welfare.

††Honda Foundation; 1977; $5,000,000;* Convenes a series of international symposiums ("Discoveries") on technology and society.

††Hoso Bunka Foundation; 1974; $52,610,000;* Provides financial assistance for research and development of broadcast technology and receiving equipment, the promotion of international cooperation in broadcasting, and so forth.

††Imai Memorial Charitable Trust for Overseas Cooperation; 1977; $870,000; Provides financial and material assistance to promote education and medical care in developing countries in general and to victims of natural disasters in developing countries.

Isetan Foundation; 1963; $570,000; Awards scholarships to Japanese nationals for university study in Japan and to those who wish to study overseas, and provides financial assistance to Japanese researchers engaged in the study of commerce.

Ishibashi Foundation; 1956; $20,990,000;* Operates the Bridgestone Museum (Tokyo) and the Ishibashi Museum (Kurume city, Fukuoka Prefecture) and sponsors fine arts lectures.

Ishizaka Foundation; 1976; $2,430,000;* Provides scholarships for Japanese undergraduate and graduate students in foreign universities and for foreign students in Japanese universities and sponsors lectures and symposiums that contribute to international cultural and educational interchange.

†§Iwatani Naoji Foundation; 1973; $10,870,000;* Provides grants for research and development projects in science and technology and provides aid to promote the international exchange of science and technology.

Japan Coca-Cola Bottlers Scholarship Fund; 1970; $2,420,000;* Provides scholarships for academically talented, financially needy students and provides guidance for scholarship recipients.

Japan Economic Research Foundation; 1976; $700,000; Provides grants for research in economics and related disciplines and provides financial aid for international exchange required by such research.

Table 1. *Continued*

†‡§ ‖ Japan Foundation; 1972; $206,520,000;* Invites individuals to Japan and sends Japanese abroad for the purpose of cultural exchange, provides assistance to Japanese studies and language programs abroad and to activities that promote international cultural exchange, and so forth.

†‡Japan Heart Foundation; 1970; $1,480,000; Provides grants for the research of heart and blood vessel disease and provides financial aid for the publication of research findings on the heart and blood vessels.

†Japan Securities Scholarship Foundation; 1973; $10,870,000;* Provides scholarships and provides financial aid for research in the arts and sciences.

†Japan Shipbuilding Industry Foundation; 1962; $251,300,000;* Promotes shipbuilding, shipbuilding-related industries, activities aimed at prevention of maritime disasters, and general public-interest activities.

†‡§ ‖ Japan Society for the Promotion of Science; 1967; annual budget $12,520,000;* Provides assistance for international joint research projects that promote international academic exchange, provides fellowships, invites foreign researchers, sends Japanese researchers abroad, and disseminates academic information.

Japan-U.S. Scholarship Foundation; 1966; $1,350,000; Awards scholarships and research grants.

‡Japanese Organization for International Cooperation in Family Planning; 1968; $740,000; Provides grants for research on family planning in developing countries and cooperates with international organizations and governmental organizations in Asia.

†‡§ ‖ JEC Fund: Commemorative Association for the Japan World Exposition, 1970; 1971; $67,390,000;* Gives awards and provides assistance for international projects relating to cultural exchange and friendship, academic and educational cooperation, social education for youth, medicine, health and hygiene, social welfare, and the preservation of nature and the human environment.

†‡Kajima Foundation; 1976; $3,260,000;* Provides grants for scientific research, awards prizes for superior research in the sciences, and provides support for international exchange in the sciences.

Kashiyama Scholarship Foundation; 1977; $870,000; Awards scholarships to college students and counsels scholarship recipients.

Kawakami Foundation; 1957; $1,300,000; Provides financial assistance for research and sponsors essay contests.

Table 1. *Continued*

Kitano Lifelong Integrated Education Foundation; 1975; $870,000; Provides aid for activities, investigation, and research concerning lifelong integrated education.

Kurata Foundation; 1967; $3,910,000;* Provides financial assistance for basic and applied research in science and technology, particularly in the areas of electrical engineering, mechanical engineering, and chemical engineering.

Marubeni Foundation; 1974; $8,040,000;* Provides financial assistance for projects and research in social welfare, culture, and education.

†§Matsumae International Foundation; 1979; $1,740,000;* Provides fellowships for senior foreign researchers to conduct research in Japan, especially in natural science, medicine, and engineering.

Matsushita Audio-Visual Education Foundation; 1973; $2,000,000; Provides financial assistance to researchers in audiovisual education and holds audiovisual education study sessions to teach educators.

†Mitsubishi Bank Foundation; 1981; $8,700,000;* Provides grants for activities to promote international exchange, international understanding, and education of internationally minded people.

†Mitsubishi Foundation; 1969; $19,570,000;* Provides grants to people conducting academic research and gives financial assistance for social welfare projects.

Mitsui Seimei Social Welfare Foundation; 1967; $960,000; Educates the public about health care and health improvement, and undertakes research and cooperates in activities concerned with disease prevention, the improvement of physical health, and so forth.

†§Naito Foundation; 1969; $1,910,000; Provides grants for scientific research related to the treatment and prevention of disease.

†‡ ‖ National Institute for Research Advancement; 1974; $60,870,000;* Conducts its own research, delineates areas of research that are deputed to other research institutions, and tries to develop and maintain close contact with research institutions abroad.

Nippon Life Insurance Foundation; 1979; $16,520,000;* Provides assistance and conducts research activities for youth and senior citizens and activities that improve the natural environment.

Nissan Science Foundation; 1974; $18,350,000;* Provides grants to institutions and individuals engaged in research, particularly in the natural sciences, and presents recommendations to researchers for outstanding achievements in the arts and sciences, particularly in the natural sciences.

Table 1. *Continued*

†‡Niwano Peace Foundation; 1978; $8,910,000;* Promotes research and other activities that serve the cause of peace, based upon a religious spirit, in such fields as philosophy and thought, science, and education.

†§Rotary Yoneyama Memorial Foundation, Inc.; 1967; $1,220,000; Provides scholarships primarily for Asian students and maintains contact with scholarship recipients and their sponsoring Rotary clubs.

Saito Memorial Fund for Research Advancement of Prestressed Concrete Technology; 1977; $400,000; Provides financial assistance for research on prestressed concrete and related technology.

Sanwa Midori Fund; 1971; $3,160,000;* Plants trees in order to improve the natural environment, provides aid for the development of pollution-prevention technology, and conducts survey research and provides consultant services for pollution problems.

Sony Foundation of Science Education; 1972; $3,850,000;* Provides financial assistance for the promotion of science education in elementary and junior high schools and provides aid for research on educational developments.

†‡Suntory Foundation; 1979; $3,170,000;* Provides grants, awards prizes to young specialists in the arts, politics, and economics, and holds international symposiums.

Takahashi Foundation; 1972; $3,040,000; Provides aid for survey research concerning the industrial economy and for experimental research in industrial technology.

Takeda Medical Research Foundation; 1977; $100,000; Provides financial assistance for research concerning basic and clinical studies on the prevention and treatment of metabolic disorders of old age.

Tokai Foundation; 1975; $2,730,000; Provides aid for projects, surveys, and research that improve the natural, living, and cultural environments.

Tokyo Kaijo Kagami Memorial Foundation; 1925; $1,170,000; Offers scholarships, and provides assistance for scholarly research and survey research of industry.

Tokyu Foundation for a Better Environment; 1974; $1,040,000; Provides financial assistance for research dealing with the relationship between industrial activities and the Tama River, the elimination of pollution of the Tama River, and water utilization in the Tama River.

†§Tokyu Foundation for Inbound Students; 1975; $1,040,000; Provides scholarships, rents housing to scholarship recipients, and counsels scholarship recipients.

Table 1. *Continued*

Toray Science Foundation; 1960; $8,080,000;* Provides aid to research institutes, individual researchers, educational institutions, and educators and students in science and technology.

†‡Toyota Foundation; 1974; $43,480,000;* Provides grants for research and projects related to the human and natural environments, education and culture, and social welfare in Japan and abroad, especially in Southeast Asia.

†Twenty-First Century Culture and Science Foundation; 1979; $2,790,000;* Provides grants for research and projects related to economics, society, and culture; and provides support for inviting foreign researchers to Japan and sending Japanese researchers abroad.

Vehicle Racing Memorial Foundation; 1975; $21,390,000; Provides additional funds for the maintenance and management of those facilities supported in part by grants from the Japan Bicycle Racing Association and the Japan Auto Race Association.

Yamamuro Memorial Society; 1953; $1,480,000; Awards scholarships and provides financial assistance for scholarly research, especially on financial conditions.

†§Yoshida Foundation for Science and Technology; 1975; $3,260,000;* Provides grants for research in science and technology, provides financial aid to researchers for overseas training or research activities, and invites foreign researchers to Japan.

†‡§Yoshida International Education Foundation; 1964; $1,430,000; Provides financial aid for research on both Japanese and foreign education, the arts and sciences, and culture and cooperates in international student exchange.

Source: Tadashi Yamamoto, *Philanthropy in Japan: A Summary Report on the Survey on Japanese Foundations* (Tokyo: Japan Center for International Exchange, 1978).
*Endowment amount has been updated as of August 1980; exchange rate: U.S. $1 = ¥230.
†Provides grants for Third World–related activities.
‡Engages in international grant making.
§Provides scholarships for foreign students and invites foreign scholars to Japan.
‖Semigovernmental.

country in Southeast Asia several years ago, he said to me, "With such a small grant budget, the Toyota Foundation will not be able to be effective. If you made one grant to the Asian Institute of Technology, your grant budget would be exhausted." I thought then that from the viewpoint of quantity, what he said might have been right, but that small grants can produce unexpectedly good results if a program is well conceived and effectively managed. Large foundations can support projects conducted by governments or regional bodies in Southeast Asia or by international organizations. They can be very helpful in the development of people by providing fellowships, and they can support universities to establish new departments. It seems to me that small foundations can leave such programs to large foundations and government agencies, and that they should focus on other types of programs. Small foundations can make contributions in supporting projects conducted at local universities, projects that change the conventional flow of information, and projects related to national studies that would enhance a sense of identity and pride in people; they can also provide seed money for projects that have some risk in the beginning but great potential.

Considering the history of Japan's modernization—its rapid transformation from a feudal system to a modern industrialized state and the great difficulties encountered in this process—it is easy for us to understand the anguish of Southeast Asian countries in the course of modernization. I have given a lengthy account of Japanese history in the early part of this essay in order to illustrate the similarities between the Japanese experience and the situation in Southeast Asia now. Of course, the two situations are not exactly the same, and it is doubtful that the direction Japan had to choose would be the most suitable one for Southeast Asian countries today.

Regardless of the direction taken by individual countries, small foundations can make contributions in the various fields mentioned earlier, and their activities can encourage rather than endanger healthy modernization. Of course, when programs are conducted in Southeast Asia, they should be initiated on the basis of the needs of the countries in question. It is important not to force programs when people do not feel the need for them or when they are not ready for them. Another important point for small foundations is that they should pay more attention to people than to organizations.

Since the size of a foundation determines the type of programs suitable for it, cooperation among foundations should be considered carefully. Foundations of a similar size can provide joint funding. Large foundations can take over successful programs supported to the extent of their funding capabilities by small foundations and conduct them on a larger scale. Foundations of various sizes can support different types of projects within a program. Thus, in order to enable cooperation among foundations, it is most important for foundations first of all to exchange information.

Lastly, I would like to introduce the activities of the Toyota Foundation. The national division of the Toyota Foundation makes grants in the fields of environment, social welfare, and education and culture to projects conducted by Japanese nationals and by people who can complete the Japanese-language grant application form. It also makes grants to projects in the humanities, to projects related to conservation of the historical environment, and to people who are engaged in Third World area studies. The foundation's articles of endowment stipulate that the international division will provide grants in the Third World. Since the Toyota Foundation is a small foundation with a limited budget, its international division is presently focusing on grants made to projects conducted by Southeast Asians in Southeast Asia. In general, international division grants are made in the fields of environment, social welfare, education and culture, and education of youth; however, since other foreign, international, and Japanese funding agencies place a high priority on science and technology, agriculture, forestry, fisheries, medicine, and the social sciences, many of the Toyota Foundation's international division grants are made to projects in the humanities. There is a growing need for projects of this sort, and an increasing number of young researchers at local universities are interested in conducting them, but funding for such work is not easily available.

For example, we have supported such projects as the inventory and microfilming of old manuscripts, the compilation of a dialect dictionary, studies of architectural history, the compilation of an inventory of ancient towns, studies of mural paintings as cultural assets, and studies on the preservation of cultural heritages. We have also supported projects related to the education of youth. Most of these projects have been conducted by young, active scholars at local universities. Aside from the grants just mentioned, we support the compilation of dictionaries that will facilitate translation from Southeast Asian languages into Japanese, and we provide fellowships for Japanese scholars engaged in Third World area studies to encourage them to become bridges between Japan and the Third World.

Along with these programs, we have a special program called the "Know Our Neighbors" Translation-Publication Program in Japan, which aims to create a reverse flow of information in the humanities and social sciences. With the cooperation of Southeast Asian scholars, writers, and professionals, the foundation compiles a list of recommended works of literature and social science that Southeast Asians wish to introduce to general readers in Japan. After identifying suitable translators, Japanese trade publishers produce these works in Japanese with the aid of translation grants from the Toyota Foundation. Presently works from Thailand, Burma, Indonesia, Malaysia, Singapore, and the Philippines are included in this program. What distinguishes the program from similar ones is that Southeast Asians initially compile the list of recommended works, the books are published not by the Toyota Foundation but by organizations in the Japanese private sector, and the works are translated directly from the original Southeast Asian languages into Japanese.

The foundation produces a newsletter in both Japanese and English featuring the titles receiving translation grants and distributes this newsletter free of charge. This illustrated newsletter includes synopses of the works, brief accounts of the authors, essays written by the translators, and responses from Japanese readers. The English edition of the first newsletter, *The Toyota Foundation Occasional Report No. 1,* was sent to interested people in Southeast Asia, Europe, and the United States. We have received favorable letters from U.S. universities expressing appreciation of our efforts. Correspondents thought the *Occasional Report* was valuable because information on Southeast Asia, especially on works written in Southeast Asian languages recounting the life of local people, is not easily available. Southeast Asians commented to us that the *Occasional Report* was very useful because it provided them with firsthand information on their neighboring countries.

In 1982 we launched the "Know Our Neighbors" Translation-Publication Program in Southeast Asia to support the translation and the publication of Japanese works in Thai, Malaysian, and Indonesian. The titles for translation and publication are selected from Southeast Asian viewpoints, which are different from those of Westerners. In the beginning there may be cases in which works already available in English will be translated into Thai and Malaysian, but our ultimate aim is to support the Thai and Malaysian publication of works translated directly from Japanese. It might be far easier to translate from English versions, but we wish to promote direct communication from Japanese to Southeast Asian languages. In 1983 we also launched the Southeast Asian "Know Our Neighbors" Translation-Publication Program to promote the translation of Southeast Asian works into other Southeast Asian languages. This program currently supports a Thai project to translate works in other Southeast Asian languages and publish them in Thai.

The "Know Our Neighbors" Translation-Publication program is a small attempt at cooperation with people in the Third World in an effort to gain insights that are important in learning about the values, ideas, and aspirations of other cultures. However, we hope that this experiment will have an impact on the present information flow and also contribute to clarification of different viewpoints from the West.

10 / Foundations and Cultural Development of the Third World

FRANCIS X. SUTTON

This final essay explores the attractions and pitfalls of cultural efforts in the developing world. A veteran of nearly three decades of founda-tion service, Francis X. Sutton stresses the need to mesh work in the humanities with other programmatic goals and to respect the dictates of national sovereignty. He traces U.S. foundations' historical interest in the Third World, underscoring the need for ongoing attention to cultural preservation in less-developed countries.

HAZARDS AND ATTRACTIONS OF CULTURAL ENTERPRISE

One must approach the subject of this essay warily: What busi-ness of ours is the cultural development of the Third World? The very term *Third World* reminds us of an avoidance of allegiance that often seems a principled opposition. We live in a time when authenticity ranks with the highest of values and cultural imperi-alism is a deadly sin. Enterprises of disinterested, scholarly, or philanthropic interest in cultures from the outside seem increas-ingly freighted with suspicion. The service of imperialism is detected in anthropology, and condescending "orientalism" in philological and historical scholarship. Cultural development—if the language is acceptable at all—is seen as a delicate and strictly national enterprise or one that must at most find external collab-oration and supports within the ambit of the Third World. And in latter-day disillusionment or fatigue with the idea of develop-ment, the very conception of "cultural development" raises the guards of those who suspect some merely bureaucratic or tech-nocratic enterprise or the instrumental subjugation of culture to the development process.

Thus, it is not obvious that the foundations, any more than other outsiders, are to be welcomed with trust or enthusiasm when they take an interest in cultural development of the Third

World. Even if they keep their distance and devote themselves to sustaining their own nations' resources of scholarship and connoisseurship on other cultures, they may not be free from charges of intrusion, of condescension, or even of encouraging pillage. We must remember these resistances and suspicions at the outset, because the attractiveness and the rightness of concerns with preservation of the diversity of human cultures, and with efforts to make them known and appreciated beyond their indigenous homes, seem so manifest. But this is nothing unusual for foundations. We always have the problem of finding roles in which we can be effective in a practical way, and we also have a need to define what is proper and legitimate for us to do, particularly when we venture beyond home grounds.

We are, of course, in a long-established and continuing enterprise. Before trying to say what foundations can and ought to do for cultural development in the Third World in the coming years, we ought to have in mind at least a general conspectus of what we have done.

HISTORICAL BACKGROUND

Anyone who has ever groped through the reports or files of foundations knows that it is hazardous to try to say either what they were trying to do or what they in fact have done. There is an abundance of reporting on the support that was actually given but, as historians and program evaluators regularly complain, much less on the analytical or philosophical reasons for undertaking such actions, and there are perhaps even worse difficulties in trying to decipher what the effects of foundation grants have been. There is a further constraint in the limited range of knowledge any one of us can bring to the foundation scene. My own acquaintance is of course best with my own institution, the Ford Foundation; less good with other U.S. and European foundations; and very imperfect indeed on the foundations that have been growing up in Japan, elsewhere in East Asia, and in other parts of the world. We all know that the vast majority of foundations concentrate on local and specialized interests, and the numbers that reach out to international interests are small indeed.

This pattern is characteristic not only of U.S. and European foundations but also of those in Latin America and other parts of the Third World where museums and other cultural institutions have been supported by local wealth, with only a few exceptions like the Aga Khan Foundation or the Mendoza Foundation taking on wider concerns. It must, however, be remembered that the local support of cultural activities by foundations in Western countries frequently has a certain connection with the cultures of the Third World. Support of the humanities and arts by U.S. foundations currently runs about $210 million a year, the greater part of it for the arts.[1] This extensive and important support of museums, performing arts institutions, and some academic and scholarly activities promotes attention to the cultures of the Third World in many parts of the United States.

The minority of foundations which take a national and international concern in their programs have had broad dealings with research and scholarship, public affairs, and development. The arts and humanities have had some place in all of these three areas of programmatic interest, although typically a rather minor one. The categories are of course not mutually exclusive. Some of the support of research and scholarship has been incidental to the latter two areas, and of course concerns with development of the Third World have been linked to concerns with foreign policy and international understanding. In the United States the lack, until quite recently, of public support for the humanities and social sciences left large scope for private support of these activities through universities and other centers of learning. The social sciences have always bulked larger than the arts and humanities in the interests of U.S. foundations, no doubt because of the pragmatic concern with evident social problems which has been so prominent in the history of American philanthropy.

Both the Rockefeller Foundation and the Ford Foundation have, nevertheless, provided large sums with the explicit aim of advancing the arts and humanistic scholarship. Through its arts and humanities programs, the Ford Foundation committed a total of such support through 1980 which amounted to approximately $294 million for the arts and $67 million for the humanities, very largely in the United States. Insofar as these commitments brought support or attention to the cultures of the Third World, they did so mostly incidentally in the context of supporting the arts and humanities in the United States. Ford's organization has been such that its concerns with Third World cultures have largely come in other program contexts and purposes, as described below. The Rockefeller Foundation program in Arts, Humanities and Contemporary Values (with 1980 commitments of $6.2 million), and its predecessors under different labels, have supported a wide array of cultural activities in the United States and internationally. In keeping with Rockefeller's strong leaning to organization by function or subject matter, interests in Third World cultures appear to have been rather more closely linked with U.S. program interests than in Ford's practice.[2] The Andrew W. Mellon Foundation, which devotes large resources to the arts and humanities, is the most important U.S. foundation in the field, but it explicitly disclaims international interests.

Looking at the U.S. foundations' explicit commitments to the arts and humanistic scholarship does, however, give a much too modest impression of the encouragement they have given to study and appreciation of the cultures of the Third World. Far and away the largest support of the Ford Foundation to such study has come through the more than $300 million we have devoted to the support of international studies in the United States. Begun in the early 1950s, this program reached its peak in the years 1965–67, when nearly $120 million were committed. Some of these funds were devoted to the study of Europe, East and West, but the great bulk was spent on studies of the Third World (including of course Latin America). Not all the funds were expended in the United States; some parts of the foundation's programs provided comparable support in Europe and elsewhere. But the main expenditures were in the United States, in keeping with the basic motivation, which was to equip the United States for a better understanding and competence in dealing with the wide range of national responsibilities which were felt following the Second World War. The main emphasis was on understanding the contemporary societies, and this goal implied a vigorous effort to develop social scientific studies of other countries. But history and language were inevitably very important, and a large fraction—hard to estimate accurately but certainly not less than one-third of the funds—was devoted to the humanities and indeed the arts.

Rockefeller and Carnegie antedated and complemented the Ford Foundation in these efforts, and in more recent years, as the Ford Foundation commitments have fallen sharply, there have been important new contributions by Mellon, Hewlett, Tinker, and some others. In company with large inputs from state, federal, and other resources, these funds have stimulated the development of major area studies centers in U.S. universities, and a great cadre of area specialists has come into existence. National programs to provide field experience for budding specialists, particularly the Foreign Area Fellowship Program managed by the Social Science Research Council and the American Council of Learned Societies, have complemented multimillion dollar grants to individual universities. A great stream of activity in research, publication, seminar and conference activity, and curricular attention to the Third World has resulted. For some areas of the world, for example, Southeast Asia and Africa, the research and publication of U.S. and other scholars have quite overwhelmed any output of indigenous scholarship for a good many years. In effect, this has been a continuation of patterns characteristic of the colonial era, when study and interpretation of cultural traditions were nearly a monopoly of outsiders. The problems inherent in a situation like this one are manifest. On the other hand, it is also evident that resources of great potential for cultural development in the Third World have been built up in the universities and research centers of the United States, and in their vast scholarly product.

The hope that a better understanding of countries around the world will contribute to better foreign policy has extended broadly to the hope that it will contribute to a more secure and peaceable international order. These wider concerns logically imply an interest in exchanges and symmetrical growth of international understanding among nations. The foundations have of course supported a great deal of international study by Third World nationals. Most of it has been in a context of development interests to which we must turn.

The familiar description of countries of the Third World as "developing nations" is a description some foundations have taken seriously. We at Ford have joined in the efforts that have gone on since the Second World War under various etiquettes as "technical assistance," "development assistance," or "development cooperation," and we have generally followed the rules and conceptions which have been international orthodoxy in these efforts. That is to say, we have tried to bring useful assistance that does not violate national sovereignty and is neutral in the sense that it carries no requirements of political or cultural commitment. The ideal of "aid without strings" is of course an ideal, imperfectly realized in practice. There is typically a great rhetorical emphasis on the initiative and agreement of nationals within their own countries, and quite honest effort not to make deliberate intrusions. Some cultural impact is certainly inevitable, but the broad tendency has been to emphasize the neutral, the technical, and the manifestly "practical."

The great bulk of development assistance to the Third World has thus been inhibited in showing any very deliberate or manifest concern with cultural matters. While large effort has been committed to education, little of it has been directly or explicitly devoted to the arts or humanities, and the foundations have generally conformed to this pattern. But there can be no doubt that foundation efforts in university development, in the encouragement of educational research, in technical assistance to educational planning, in the development of curriculum centers, and in the support of materials development for schools have exercised important cultural influences. University development has been the largest category of activity in the Third World for the Ford Foundation and for the Carnegie Corporation, and indeed bulks very large in Rockefeller's historical record; the prevailing views on its proper character have been such as to encourage attention to what may be called cultural development. If universities are to be adapted to their settings and not to be simple copies of institutions elsewhere, what they do must be based upon knowledge and appreciation of the character of their countries; hence much emphasis on the universities' responsibility for building knowledge of the history and linguistic and cultural variety of their countries and for shaping their curricula accordingly, and hence the provision of many foundation grants in support of institutes of African or Southeast Asian studies, or the like, and for research and program development of many sorts.

In recent years there has been a regrettable decline in attention to universities in Third World countries, as indeed to education generally. For some fifteen years, the educational programs of the Ford Foundation led to a strong interest in Third World languages and the problems of combining them with English or French in school systems. Other examples of the attention to cultural development through education could be cited, but it must be remembered that they are now much reduced through a general shift away from the past strong engagement with education.

Cultural development as such has, despite inhibitions, had some recognition as a significant and legitimate part of foundation development programs. Foundation interests have focused particularly on cultural preservation and the training of people from Third World countries to carry out such work. Over the years, the Ford Foundation committed something approaching $10 million to these purposes, particularly in South and Southeast Asia, and the Rockefeller Foundation, the JDR 3rd Fund, and others have been active too.

Exchanges have served the purposes of cultural development and wider purposes in international relations as well. Looking back to the 1950s, one finds ambitions to project the cultural image of the United States and to provide an intellectual defense of the free world that now seem almost embarrassingly straightforward. In the 1950s the Ford Foundation went heavily into the support of American studies abroad and founded Intercultural Publications, which through its *Perspectives USA* tried to show that the United States was not only rich and powerful but "cultured" too. Major support of the Congress for Cultural Freedom came somewhat later, when genuine foundation support was needed to replace "conduits." Not much of this multimillion dollar expenditure was directed to the Third World. Europe had the lion's share, but there was some serious attention (particularly through the congress and its successor's publications and cultural centers) to Asia, Africa, and Latin America. Other foundations seem to have kept rather more discreet distances from explicit ideological or political objectives but to have shared in support of American studies abroad or of programs of international cultural exchange.

The telling of these various activities runs on, even without much pausing for enlivening illustration. But I do not want to give the impression that I think the record of the foundations in their service and attention to Third World cultures has been particularly brave and laudable. The record looks best where foundations seem to feel most comfortable—close to home. It is in their support of research and scholarship in their own countries that they have done the most for Third World cultures.[3] Arts and humanities programs generally seem to give at best modest and incidental attention to the Third World. It is only in the contexts of other interests—building national competences for international affairs, spreading international understanding or reinforcing international ties, providing development assistance—

that more substantial attention to cultural matters has sometimes occurred. Whether the situation as it has been is about as it ought to be, or if cultures of the Third World deserve more substantive attention than they have had, is a question that requires a look at what cultural development is, how important it is, and what its needs for assistance are.

THE NATURE AND IMPORTANCE OF CULTURAL DEVELOPMENT

The explosion in Iran brought to everyone's mind an awareness of the hazards in development. A simple interpretation is that a forced pace of modernization created strains that became intolerable and burst into a passionate revival of traditions that had seemed to be fading into the past. I have neither the presumption nor the space to offer a serious analysis of the Iranian revolution. But it does seem obvious that the simple view has merits. We have always been conscious that modernization assaulted the common values and sense of personal worth of large numbers of people who were subject to it. In the Western world, efforts to understand the Nazi movement, the antipathies of right and left, or the peculiar pessimism and antinomianism of twentieth-century culture have made us conscious of the deep strains and far-reaching consequences of this process. In the years after the Second World War, the whole world became committed to modernizing development, and in the optimism that has brightened the world until the last decade, the costs of modernization have been rather little regarded. But we are now conscious that a great many of the fateful troubles of the present time are traceable thereto.

Perhaps the greatest historical features of the era since World War II have been the rise of national sovereignty throughout the world and the spread of egalitarian values on which it has been based. The right to national self-determination is at bottom a kind of collective egalitarianism, proclaiming that any sizable, coherent group claiming a territory has a right to independent and sovereign control of that territory. As always with ideological principles, rigorously logical application does not occur and there are many examples of separatism indignantly denied. The bases on which claims to be internationally recognized nation-states are in fact legitimized have been a subtle subject for scholars like Dankwart Rustow or Hugh Seton-Watson.[4] They have codified and interpreted the common observation that some nation-states have been built around a shared ethnic or cultural identity and some only around the political divisions of a colonial or imperial past. But a common element in the sweeping emergence of national sovereignties in the modern era has been a rejection of past ascendancies and a claim of previously subjugated peoples to equal regard with others in the world. It would indeed appear that the emergence of national sovereignties over a great part of the world has been as much a symbolic expression of egalitarian claims as a rational effort at the advancement of people's welfare. The claim to equal sovereign rights gains expression in the United Nations and other formal international contexts, but enormous and indeed growing inequalities persist. Before this modern era, it was not a scandal that there were rich peoples and poor peoples; nowadays gross differences are regarded as deplorable or iniquitous, and there has been general acceptance of the principle that it is the business of development to remove them. During much of the postwar era, the emphasis has been on internal national development; currently the emphasis among Third World countries is heavily on fundamental reform and the establishment of a "new international economic order."

National sovereignty has thus come to the fore as an expression of claims for basic rights extended to all humanity. It implies on the one hand a necessary emphasis on distinctiveness or uniqueness and on the other hand a regard to international comparisons, solidarities, or oppositions. National loyalties must be nurtured by a sense of common identity. Resources for this identity may be found partly in a common historical experience—say, in deeds of the struggle for independence. But there is characteristically a need to reach beyond, into evidences of a common cultural heritage and its contemporary development. Hence it is normal for a modern government to have a ministry of culture or some functional equivalent. The tasks of such ministries are notoriously difficult ones. They must be loyal to the modernizing aspirations of their countries, while nurturing and protecting traditions that suffer under the assaults of modernity and may be sources of internal division. Modernity characteristically involves cultural imports which must somehow be received without denigration of what is authentically indigenous.

People who are capable of guiding processes of this sort with imagination and sensibility are not easy to find. This is intellectual business, and intellectuals are notoriously ambivalent and fractious, given more easily to opposition than to loyalties. (One remembers Edward Shils's depictions of the Indian intellectuals or Bernard Pares's of the intellectuals in czarist Russia.) The revulsion of Western intellectuals against anything smacking of "official culture" provides a model Third World intellectuals find hard to ignore. Many Third World countries are too small to have the abundance of talent from which capable leadership for the building of national cultures can readily be drawn. Even India and China, backed by great civilizations, have had enormous difficulties. In the best of circumstances, the hazards in the way of creative effort are formidable, and as we are all aware, the difficulties of maintaining political stability and a confident national spirit commonly lead to intolerance and repression.

All these difficulties being recognized, the task of building national cultural identities is not a bootless one. It is indeed a necessary and noble task, of the greatest importance to the future well-being of the world. Whatever the frightening and disagreeable features of nationalism in the modern world, we are not going to be rid of it in the discernible future. We will all continue to have fateful identities as citizens of national states, and it is urgently important that these identities not be sources of disgust or despair. Pride or satisfaction in national identity of course depends upon much more than cultural characteristics. It is inescapably linked to national power and wealth, but it would be deadly for national pride to be based solely on these comparisons. Fortunately it is never so; our patriotism is built on a sense of distinctive and prized qualities in our fellow citizens' styles of life, the expressiveness and comforting familiarity of language, our common memories and values, and much else. The task of cultural development in a careening pace of change is the delicate one of extending and strengthening a web of common culture in which successive generations of citizens can move with a sense of support and comfort and without binding constraints.

Much of cultural development is beyond the reach of any plan or policy. It must be an organic growth in which the activities of diversely placed individuals and groups respond to their needs and circumstances. But there are some elements of this process which seem evidently necessary and can be helped by deliberate efforts and provision of resources. One such element is *cultural preservation*. Parts of a culture and indeed whole traditions are constantly being left behind and lost. The winnowing is perhaps as normal as the fading of overloaded memories or the unique qualities of a generation. Not all of a cultural heritage can or should be preserved. In the alarm at the rapid disappearance of cultures we sometimes encounter passionate appeals for recording and collection of whole cultural patrimonies.[5] The aspiration is an impossible one, but there are unquestionably very grave problems of cultural preservation among a great many of the Third World nations. They characteristically lack the resources for research, collection, recording, and storing traditions and artifacts. In the ambition to modernize, many older practices and ways of life are rejected, and the beliefs, ceremonies, art styles, and artifacts that went with them are allowed to disappear. In some cases authoritarian ideological governments attempt to blot out whole historical experiences or cultural traditions.

To accept some losses as inevitable is not to accept a total disregard of the past. There must be discriminating selection of those elements of the cultural tradition that are of particular quality, importance, or continuing significance. The achievement of such discriminating preservation requires considerable resources and many sorts of talent. There must be scholars, technicians, artists, intellectuals, educators, and indeed cultural propagandists who devote themselves to sorting and saving. There must be institutions through which these people can work and the resources to sustain them. The scholarly disciplines, many of the techniques, and some of the resources must in typical cases come from abroad. And in some sad cases it may be necessary to preserve cultures in exile until some destructive or resolutely narrow-minded patch of history is gone.

Preservation, of course, cannot be the whole of cultural development. National cultures must be cultures of modernity as well as tradition, and they must reconcile importations with what is authentically their own. Many countries must depend upon a foreign language as the principal language of their higher education. They must depend upon science and technology from abroad. And as they become drawn into the web of international communications, their popular culture becomes exposed to records, films, books, and periodicals that spread the modern cosmopolitan culture. The seductions of this modern cosmopolitan culture are of course enormous. It brings pleasures of sophisticated entertainment, visions of different ways of life, and incitements to consumption that threaten humiliating comparisons with what peoples have had and valued. Radical reactions against this invasion are quite possible, as Iran and the Ayatollah Khomeini have taught us. In the more common case, there is a struggle to reconcile or control.

The challenge is almost coextensive with the challenge of development itself, but there are some features of it which may be seen to be very specifically cultural. Many of them have to do with the nature and functions of the educational system and with the place of humanistic studies in them. A role for universities and colleges in providing interpretations of historical development, national and international, in the criticism and interpretation of literary and artistic products both national and international, seems patently essential and important. In fact the universities in the Third World seem now very imperfectly equipped for such large responsibilities. The traditions of European higher education on which most of the universities of the Third World have been patterned have been closer to specialized professional education than to the broad needs of liberal education which would seem to be most pertinent to these responsibilities. The slow and limited development of markets for literature and for the visual and the performing arts in most places provides limited opportunities for sophisticated responses of artists and intellectuals to the contemporary cultural scene. The interests of the external world are guided by motivations that are strongly commercial and as such more likely to promote the cosmopolitan and popular cultures than more sophisticated indigenous responses.[6] I have already remarked on the tendencies of development assistance to concentrate on technical and economic development with only rare and inhibited excursions into the arts and humanities. The overall result would appear to be an exiguity of resources for the tasks of discriminating and critical shaping of contemporary cultures that parallels the thinness of resources for cultural preservation.

In some respects, Third World nations do not have to depend upon their own resources alone but may find important help within their own regions and broader traditions. An African country can have recourse to writers, artists, scholars, and ideologists from other African countries. (Indeed, the naming of countries like Ghana or Benin shows a reach to cultural claims that are broadly African and hardly conform to the heritage of their own territories.) Much of the effort to define a cultural identity for Africans has been in broadly African terms. Similarly, in Latin America a common language and common elements of the European tradition have made possible the reinforcement of national efforts by those in other countries in the region.

The wider dependencies of cultural development provoke tense ambivalences. The most determinedly nationalistic writers and artists find themselves unconsciously addressing international audiences. (Thus, for example, Edward Shils finds the Indian nationalist Subhas Chandra Bose explaining in his writing for Indians things that Englishmen, not Indians, need to have explained.)[7] The critical and polemical writings of the Third World are full of warnings on the subtle intrusions of external standards and influences and fierce declarations on the need to root them out. But this is surely an impossible and indeed destructive counsel. The international transparencies of a modernizing world inevitably mean that cultural development must be a kind of symbiotic process engaging borrowers and lenders, models and copiers, foils and adversaries. It is of course not a comfortably symmetrical process. Great and confident nations may be rudely inattentive to nations that seem backward or inconsequential. The arrogance of the West persists, and it often takes comfortingly paternalistic forms in exhortations to be helpful in the cultural development of others.

A condescending or merely prudential Western view (that misshapen cultural development threatens world peace) bespeaks insufficient reflection on the cultural crises that now afflict the Western world. There is no Third World monopoly on crises of meaning and value. Perhaps I can let Czeslaw Milosz speak to the issue: "Yes, the Universal is devouring the Particular, our fingers are heavy with Chinese and Assyrian rings, civilizations are as short-lived as weeks of our lives, places which not long ago were celebrated as homelands under oak trees are now no more than states on a map, and each day we ourselves lose letter after letter from our names which still distinguish us from each other."[8] One could have quoted as well an Italian poet, a Harvard professor, a French philosopher, or an English critic.[9] We must all now find our way in a world where we have lost simple confidence in received and settled doctrines and ways of living; we are conscious that men and women living in other times and places have felt and thought differently and are not to be ignored or deprecated. There are of course grave temptations to arrogant myopia. The rationalizing positivism that is embedded in the modern spirit opens all of the past and present to questioning. It threatens to reduce most of the record of human striving to prejudice and error. But there is constant hesitation before this sweeping confidence in our capacities to perfect human life, and in our universalizing temper we probe in all directions for guides to meaning and satisfaction in human life. Anthropology becomes more than mere scientific curiosity, history more than tales of old ignorance and folly, and philosophy and religion are opened by concession that human vision is not confined to the West.

There are of course many levels of seriousness in the engagement we have with cultures not our own. I have recently been struck by an essay by the English literary scholar Malcolm Bradbury, telling of our exposure to "bazaars of culture without consequences" and arguing that we live in an "age of parody" because no one can be free from an awareness of styles and models from pasts and elsewheres.[10] But there are depths, too, perhaps most powerfully displayed in those unreconciled to radical secularization or de-Christianization of the West and yet conscious that the West has had no legitimate monopoly on religious experience. Thus we find that great scholar Wilfred Cantwell Smith having to say: "I do not say that God was revealed in Jesus Christ just like that, absolutely, impersonally, and I suggest that it is not a good thing to say. I say that God has been revealed to me in Jesus Christ, and has been to many millions of people throughout history . . . [yet] . . . God is not revealed fully in Jesus Christ to me, nor indeed to anyone that I have met; or that my historical studies have uncovered."[11]

There is something more than a little dismaying in coming to believe that carvings from New Guinea, oral traditions from Indians of Colombia, and the Upanishads must be brought into some vast collage for our modern culture. There is a vastness and variety to human experience and culture that only heedless enthusiasts for international openness can view without concern. Just as some principles of selection and critical winnowing are necessary in the domestic cultural development of nations, so all the world has a formidable task in maintaining openness without dispiriting confusion. The dangers of a retreat into a surly parochialism are evident unless there is some guide to what is rewarding and enlightening. Fortunately, the historical record suggests that something between promiscuous randomness and mere fads and fashions does occur. The interest of writers and artists in Japanese painting and poetry in the decades around the beginning of this century; the response to African art a little later; the interest in Indian religion from the middle of the last century down to our own time—all these seem to have been movements in which discerning Westerners brought new stimuli and creativity to Western art and thought by fixing on particular cultural traditions from elsewhere. It is evident that such currents of cultural influence and their contributions to cultural development have depended upon scholarly and creative spirits who have had to find the resources to sustain their efforts through some means or another.

It is tempting to proclaim that the decades ahead will be an exciting era in which all the world will be engaged in a common enterprise of preserving the letters in our names, to echo Milosz, while sharing in a rich and evolving universal culture. Things will certainly not be so happy and simple. There will be confusion, miscarriages, overreachings, and lapses. One can speculate that general patterns will change as nations move through formative stages to more settled national cultural existences. The flowering of cultural activity in the crises as nations are forming may not carry on as splendidly once the crises are passed. One thinks of the great flowering of German culture in the time of Goethe, Schiller, Kant, and Beethoven as the German nation formed; the literary, musical, and philosophical achievements of prerevolutionary Russia; or the Indian renaissance from Ram Mohan Roy, through Vivekananda and Tagore, to Nehru and Gandhi. Moments when nations and cultures are forming are likely to have international or universal interest almost by the nature of the clashes and syntheses they involve. Even if repressive conformity does not settle down, the possibility of an inward-turning preoccupation may make nations in their more mature phases less rich focuses of wider interest. As nations of the Third World move into a more confident and settled nationhood, they may thus be less stimulating to others.

But this is very uncertain speculation. What is certain is that cultural development will matter crucially to the stability of the Third World nations and to the lives of their own citizens. And it is only slightly less certain that the enrichment of human variety and achievement that this development will bring will be important to the needs of the rest of the world. An interest in this cultural development is thus evidently of much more than benevolent or prudential character to the rest of the world. We cannot clearly anticipate what the significance will be, but our needs for meaningful experience are such that we can hardly afford to neglect whatever promises to be helpful in them.

ROLES FOR FOUNDATIONS

My effort has been to set forth what I think cultural development means, why it is important, and some of the things it requires. However brief the description, I hope it will have been evident that I perceive a serious dearth of resources in great parts of the Third World for coping with the tasks of preservation and contemporary development that are before them. In nearly all cases there are deficiencies in financial resources, institutional strengths, and trained talent. The limitations on these national resources are not likely to be removed in the near future, and postponed efforts mean threats of irreparable losses. A rich field for international assistance thus exists. As I have earlier suggested, it is unfortunately a little-worked and uncrowded field. UNESCO assumes some responsibilities, but its resources can cover only a small fraction of the needs, and national cultural relations programs are more concerned with *rayonnement* than with others' renaissance. A serious effort in cultural preservation for a sizable country ought to be a systematic one extending over several years. It should attend fundamentally to the training and development of those categories of talent necessary to the tasks of collection, recording, analysis, interpretation, and education. Even within limited fields of subject matter this is a large undertaking. Physical monuments and artifacts need the skills of archaeologists, conservators, museologists, and art historians. Music and dance require ethnomusicologists, modern performers, impresarios—the list goes on and on.

One might conclude from such reflection on the needs of cultural preservation and development that a serious approach to them is beyond the resources and likely commitments of foundations. I do not mean to draw that discouraging conclusion. It seems to me that a few foundations may be in a position to give sustained and serious attention to the cultural development of particular countries or regions. We certainly have had something of the sort for the Asian arts in the work of the JDR 3rd Fund and now of the Asian Arts Council, and we have had an approach to such efforts by the Ford Foundation in South and Southeast Asia in recent years (although Ford is very conscious of the limitations of what it has been able to do thus far). Other examples, such as the Tinker Foundation in Latin America, could be mentioned. But the principal point that I would make is that it seems likely that a foundation from abroad will attend most helpfully to cultural development of particular nations or regions when its interest is reinforced by some other program concern of the foundation.

An interest in Third World cultural development has grown up within broader interests in development assistance. But if my survey is not misleading, this concern has not in the past led to very substantial efforts, except perhaps through education. Regrettably, it does not appear to me that more substantial efforts are likely to come from such broader development interests in the future. The current involvement of foundations in Third World educational systems and institutions is now quite limited and probably declining. I could, if pressed, identify a few promising signs of a turn toward more positive undertakings, and I could enthusiastically endorse them. But I could not soberly predict a flowering of foundation support arising from this source. There must, I believe, be other and more intrinsic interests in cultural development which derive from something beyond a general concern with Third World development as such.

Most important and promising seem to me those interests that relate to needs in the foundation's home country. The support there of artistic, literary, philosophical, and scholarly activities can be variously motivated, as I have tried to show. A foundation may feel it should support work on cultures of the Third World because of a sense of their importance to its country's foreign relations, to its place in world scholarship and culture, or to its citizens' needs for esthetic experience and meaningful lives. A mix of motivations will doubtless be common, and clarity of motives may not be a great virtue, as long as the arts and humanities are left in creative freedom, and there is a sense of fundamental sharing with the Third World in the needs for cultural development.

The way in which knowledge and appreciation of Third World cultures are approached is of great importance. Accepting that a large part of the interest will focus in the foundation's home country does not imply indifference to what goes on in the Third World itself. Indeed, firsthand contact and lively collaboration such as foundations can promote would seem to be essential. The fact that we all live together in a shaky and confused world means that cultural development for any nation is not its business alone. Each nation, Third World or First, is affected by others, and the artists, intellectuals, and scholars who mediate between cultures are important to all of us. The interest in human rights and intellectual freedom has been one important recent motivation to attention to this precious band, inside and outside their native countries. It has shown the importance of material and symbolic international support in sustaining the determination and courage of those who venture to think or act as freely as honest creative effort demands. The international support that foundations can bring is easiest in the realms of pure scholarship and artistic or literary creation. But support may need at times to go beyond into the philosophical and ideological realms that the defense of freedom requires, and we should not be afraid to follow these needs as far as the tax people will let us venture.

I have not tried to minimize the hazards of cultural enterprise or to obscure the various motivations that lead foundations into them. We all like to believe that we are engaged in philanthropy with high, disinterested motives, and it is tempting to aspire to serve the arts and learning for their own pure sakes. But these things enter too intimately and urgently into public and private concerns to be kept isolated and pure. And trying to isolate them is not to serve them well. Cultural development, the West's and the Third World's, will be promoted more abundantly and persistently if we let its uses and importance be seen as essential to many purposes that move our trustees and ourselves.

NOTES

1. Figures for 1982 from the American Association of Fund-Raising Counsel, *Giving USA* (New York: American Association of Fund-Raising Counsel, 1983), pp. 23, 78.

2. Thus, for example, recent grants for U.S.-African exchanges in

the performing arts would have been actions requiring collaboration of two separate divisions of the Ford Foundation.

3. The examples I have given are parochially American. But my acquaintance with the work of foundations in other countries would seem to support the more general assertion. Recent Volkswagen and Thyssen reports, for example, show various and interesting support of German scholarship on Third World cultural subjects. Volkswagen had a program for support of research on the Contemporary Near and Middle East between 1971 and 1981 which was mostly social science but included such projects as a University of Münster study of "the Arabizing of North Africa as reflected in contemporary literature" and an exchange with Cairo on contemporary Egyptian literature. The Volkswagen Southeast Asian program, running since 1976–77, seeks to support German researchers on the region but also to build working contacts with Southeast Asian scholars and institutions, and it provides grants in Southeast Asia which do not necessarily involve collaboration with German scholars. Stiftung Volkswagenwerk, *Bericht* (Hannover: Stiftung Volkswagenwerk, 1979–80), p. 89.

4. Dankwart Rustow, *A World of Nations: Problems of Political Modernization* (Washington, D.C.: Brookings Institution, 1967); Hugh Seton-Watson, *Nations and States* (Boulder, Colo.: Westview Press, 1977).

5. See, for example, Alpha I. Sow in *Introduction à la culture africaine* (Paris: UNESCO, 1977), pp. 37–42.

6. It would not be just to overlook the impressive efforts that some publishers have made in various parts of the world to promote national literatures. Some of these efforts have no doubt been stimulated by a concern to maintain markets for school texts in European languages, but the contributions of such publishers as Oxford or Heineman to African and Asian literature have certainly been impressive. There may be comparable accompaniments of commercial interests in other fields of which I am personally not aware.

7. Edward Shils, "The Culture of the Intellectual," *Sewanee Review* 67 (April and July 1959): 28.

8. Czeslaw Milosz, "From the Rising of the Sun," part 3 of *Bells in Winter* (New York: Ecco Press, 1978), p. 50.

9. Or, perhaps better, the great Mexican poet and seer Octavio Paz. One choice among many would be *The Labyrinth of Solitude* (New York: Grove Press, 1961), pp. 170–73.

10. Malcolm Bradbury, "An Age of Parody," *Encounter* 55, no. 1 (July 1980): 36.

11. Wilfred Cantwell Smith, *Toward a World Theology* (New York: Macmillan Co., 1981), quoted in a review in the *Times Literary Supplement* 4 (September 1981): 996.

11 / Discussions

The second round of discussions underscored the range of shared concerns among members of the foundation community and placed them within an international context. As Meriel Wilmot of Australia's Myer Foundation explained, "I traveled thirteen thousand miles hoping to find some solutions, and instead I find the same problems, but on a larger scale." The changing role of foundations in a period of governmental retrenchment was of particularly vital interest. How can cultural endeavors—and the work of other nonprofit enterprises as well—be strengthened and maintained in an era of dwindling resources? How widespread are multinational cooperative ventures among foundations, and how welcome? Are the more-favored countries interested in helping developing nations, and how high on the list of activities to be supported would the humanities be? Questions such as these formed the parameters of the ensuing discussions.

FOUNDATIONS, GOVERNMENT, AND ALTERNATIVE MEANS OF SUPPORT

The impact of worldwide inflation, recession, and governmental retrenchment has clearly reverberated throughout the international foundation community. As Meriel Wilmot so perceptively noted, "In many ways foundations have to put up with working as a servant of government. But the cost is getting very high—so high that it can modify policies." For example, "Ten years ago one could say, 'This is a very exciting idea. Let's stimulate these people to develop it further.' " It is no longer possible to make this statement, argued Wilmot, "because there is a 90 percent chance that the government will no longer pick it up."

Ronald Tress of the Leverhulme Trust in Great Britain translated this phenomenon into what he termed the plight of the "pioneers and pensioners." How, he asked, "can foundations maintain their initiative and pioneering functions when there is no public authority ready to assume responsibility for what has been established?" How can they "maintain the best of the older projects, and at the same time encourage new things that are coming along? How can foundations continue to innovate and sponsor new undertakings with an unchanged budget, but not let sink the good things which they have sponsored? This is likely to become a perpetual problem."

"Is it fair to grantees," queried Wilmot, "to give them a two-year allowance, and then see the whole thing collapse because the government will not pick it up? One is forced into the position of making very hard choices, of saying, 'All right, I'll give you one or two years' worth of support, but I really do not know whether you will be able to get government funding. Are you prepared to take the risk?' "

"This is a problem we are all grappling with," commented Ian Lancaster of the Gulbenkian Foundation. "For years foundations in Britain operated in an unspoken partnership with government, starting things and then waiting for government to take them up. Now we see the danger that innovation is genuinely at risk. With all the constraints on government expenditures, all the problems facing the Arts Council this year, it is very important to the continued progress of the arts that things which are good be enabled to continue, even if it means making harsh decisions at the governmental or quasi-governmental level about who gets scarce resources. New ideas must not be allowed to languish because old ideas still need support."

Waldemar Nielsen of the Aspen Institute addressed the problem of the "pioneers and pensioners" from a U.S. perspective, painting an exceedingly gloomy picture in the process:

The next few years, whether that is three years or five years or the whole decade, are certainly going to be a period of severe stress and of limited or no growth, or even a decline in the areas of funding. And at the same time all of these societal pressures and societal expectations will continue. Foundations in that period are certainly going to hear with increasing shrillness appeals for help from institutions that feel that they are in acute difficulty in maintaining what they regard as essential services. Not all of these appeals can be ignored, nor should they be. There are certainly going to be situations in all of our countries where certain institutions are of such value, such critical importance to the society, that one cannot exclude the salvaging or rescuing or sustenance role. This flood of appeals is growing and will continue to grow not only in quantity but in urgency.

One of the most difficult problems that foundations will have to face, again and again, every day in this period of austerity, is this continuous choice of maintaining some kind of a balance in their activities, some kind of balance in their notion of their own social role, between the salvaging and sustenance of endangered existing institutions and supporting new initiatives, creative developments, even though in many cases this is only going to aggravate the difficulties of struggling institutions trying to solve their own terrible problems of where to cut and how to distribute their increasingly inadequate funds in relation to the demands upon them.

Nonetheless, Nielsen insisted, "foundations can be very important creative forces in the humanities as well as in other fields if they can strike the right balance between these very conflicting demands."

Ronald Tress maintained that "there are two sets of specific problems arising out of the cutbacks." One is "the lack of recruitment among young people, and an aging population of teachers, which does not bode well for the continuation of the subjects. That in itself is a problem which the foundations might tackle. The second is the need for innovation in subject matter. Here I think the role of the foundation is what it has been, but with a very powerful conditional clause added: that we will fund the innovation, the new initiative, for a restricted period, but there has got to be a firm commitment on the part of the beneficiaries that they will take it over eventually, because they cannot be assured of continuous funds."

Meriel Wilmot illustrated some of Tress's points with examples drawn from her experiences in Australia. "In the 1960s we established a school of Oriental Studies at the University of Melbourne," she noted. "We stayed with that for eight years. Back then we could afford that. And at the end of that time the university could expect to pick it up." However, "four years ago we assisted in the establishment of a Latin American Institute at another university, pledging only a three-year grant at the outset. In the fourth year, the university people came back and said that they were unable to sustain it by themselves. They asked for additional funding, and after a great deal of discussion, we agreed to go on for one more year. But in each case, the burden fell back on the university. It was a great problem. You put the burden on the universities, forcing them to make choices of whether they will pick up the initiatives and cut back on other areas. Although foundations can initiate programs and do good work, we must also realize that we are sometimes brewing up troubles for the universities, rather than assisting them."

To this objection Tress succinctly replied, "There is no way that universities ought to be bailed out of their responsibilities by being allowed to become pensioners." Instead, they must learn to become self-supporting for, as Carnegie Corporation representative Danella Schiffer pointed out, "in getting such funds, the university is often learning to live beyond its means."

One of the major problems facing universities at the moment, noted Tress, "is the retention of minimum representation in the humanities in a range of disciplines. If there is only one department in the country in Tibetan studies, and very few students of Tibetan studies, should it be retained or not? It is a question of policy, in which finances are not the sole consideration."

Nils-Eric Svensson of the Bank of Sweden Tercentenary Foundation added the point that "this is not only a question of quantity but also of quality. Looking to ourselves as complements to the government, what are the best initiatives to take?"

Waldemar Nielsen replied, "It would be a great loss if foundations, particularly in the humanities, got themselves into a solely conservationist frame of mind."

"Clearly the economic and political climate in the 1980s throughout the world is already very different from preceding decades, and the implications for funding are profound," noted Danella Schiffer. "In the United States, for example, many nonprofits which thrived in the past now have three choices: retrenchment, merging with other similar organizations, or going out of business. What are the implications for cultural endeavors, and how can foundations respond creatively to the crisis that is before us?"

Her first suggestion was to "help scholarly pursuits become less expensive, possibly via computer technology." As she explained, "The humanities are labor-intensive enterprises, with considerable time and dollars going into research. Why can't technology help in this respect? Computers can be used to manage information. Perhaps this would be a way to get the corporate community involved, by persuading them to play a role in the extension of technology to humanistic undertakings."

"This is the kind of area where the provision of resources in kind can be very usefully explored," asserted Ian Lancaster. "We've just been doing a study on the role of computers in the management of the arts" at Gulbenkian, and "the Ford Foundation has been doing work on an income-management system for the arts, which would create a tremendous program internationally for large and small arts organizations." Moreover, the use of such technological aids "is very common in the natural sciences, where computers are brought to bear on storage and retrieval of information, problem solving, and research projects."

Although he felt that such systems might have more potential for arts management than for the humanities, W. McNeil Lowry added that "the use of computer resources and other storage information and retrieval devices is very far advanced in many countries for libraries, including humanistic libraries, periodicals, and so on. It can facilitate the better access to, and distribution of, periodicals. It can also encourage different ways of printing and circulating learned journals. This kind of collaboration and cooperation can be very fruitful and very far advanced, and I think even the more broadly scholarship-dominated associations and councils, like the American Council of Learned Societies, are working along these lines. This can be a very useful kind of cost-saving device for the humanities."

Tadashi Yamamoto of the Japan Center for International Exchange introduced a second alternative. In order to redress the "sense that there is a sort of garrison mentality, that the humanities are under siege, and having somehow to survive," scholars should turn to the marketplace, for "realistically, you have to somehow reconcile whatever you do in the humanities with the realities of the world. Philanthropic money seems to be in the decline, relatively speaking, but I think that there will be more money available in the marketplace. You might be well advised to think of taking advantage of various commercial opportunities. Trying to promote the cause of the humanities by various market mechanisms, whether it be publishing, exhibits, or whatever, is a very common thing in Japan. The defeatism I detect is based on a rather traditional approach to seed money. If you redirect your thinking to the way things now work, perhaps you don't have to be all that pessimistic." In order to take the best advantage of these resources, Yamamoto advised grant-seeking humanists to adopt "a certain entrepreneurship." As he explained, "Market mechanism aspects which are usually tied to museums can be tied to other research activities as well. For example, Japanese corporations could be used to support archaeological projects which would contain the development of discoveries in the field. It is a mistake to separate the more popular forms from scholarly research."

Ford Foundation representative Francis X. Sutton enthusiastically agreed that "for the support of the humanities and much more spectacularly for the support of the arts, the market is really terribly important. People do in fact pay for the arts and humanities, and they will continue to pay, and we ought somehow as foundations to relate to that fact." The publishing industry plays a particularly important role in the humanities. "Quite clearly," Sutton continued, "the great part of publication in the humanities is supported by the market, not by philanthropy and not by government. This is particularly true of periodicals such as the *New York Review of Books,* or the *Times Literary Supplement* in Britain, which seem to me to be some of the greatest sources of exposure to the humanities for the general population. We all have questions about the subsidy of publications, which are very important questions and need to be related to the role of markets. Do we match grants from the National Endowment for the Humanities? Do we provide subsidies for American university presses? These are immediate practical questions for everybody involved."

Perhaps the most novel suggestion was that of Belen Abreu of the Ramon Magsaysay Award Foundation in Manila, who urged the necessity of self-support. Interestingly, she used the example of her own organization, which was launched a quarter of a century earlier with a $500,000 grant from the Rockefeller Brothers Fund. The Ramon Magsaysay Award Foundation annually awards $50,000 in prizes for Asians who have "served their people with dedication." The foundation's trustees were empowered to use both the interest and the grant capital in making the awards, with the expectation that others would contribute to continue the program. The Philippine government also gave them a prime piece of real estate on a prestigious avenue. "The idea of the government was to enable us later on to put up our own building, to house the foundation and at the same time to earn income for the foundation." Much to their consternation, the trustees soon discovered that "carrying the Rockefeller name makes it too difficult to raise funds." By 1963 "there were no new funds coming in." At this point, they decided to build their own building, to generate new income, but found that "funds for buildings are not easy to come by, particularly if you want to make it economically feasible." Unable to manage with the high-interest, short-term loans which were offered them by local banks, the trustees turned instead to the Rockefeller Brothers Fund, which made a $1 million grant and loaned $2 million for construction.

"We really worked hard," Abreu recalled, and in the process "we learned what it is to administer a building." The building was finished in 1967, and the foundation has been self-supporting since 1969. The experience was a difficult lesson, but it served its students well. As Abreu explained, "It has not been easy but it has been a very good disciplinary action for those who were called upon to run the foundation. We have to earn the money to carry out our programs, and somehow that gives you an extra measure of care, of really working hard, and at the same time being worthy of the confidence your benefactors have given you. And this has been copied by other organizations in the Philippines, which pooled their resources, put up buildings, and then let the building support their programs. So now as we build up our funds, we have increased funding for our library to include educational slide shows. It is a good discipline to learn to earn the money to run the programs." And it is a discipline which might be applied to humanistic research centers.

Possibilities for international cooperation were similarly assayed. Tadashi Yamamoto strongly maintained that "the question of international foundation cooperation is an issue which is both important and necessary." As countries grow more independent, conflicts arise which feed chauvinistic elements and foster dangerous misunderstandings among nations. "Foundations are in a unique position to promote international cooperation in the humanities and other fields as well," Yamamoto noted, "because they are nonprofit, nongovernmental institutions. They do not represent vested interests." As such, they are well situated to attack common problems which transcend national bounds. Moreover, because many parts of the world presently face a period of economic nongrowth, cooperation can help foundations to conserve their limited resources and put their funds to more efficient use.

Such cooperation can take many forms, from simple information exchange among foundation personnel to jointly funded ventures. The latter technique is particularly useful in Third World areas, helping to "diffuse the potentially politicized image of foundation involvement" by distributing project responsibility across an array of nations. As the number of funders increases, so do the scope and scale of the programs they can initiate. In Japan the lure of collaborative funding often helps to draw donors into areas which they might not otherwise approach, including international programs for Southeast Asia. The results can be mutually beneficial. As Yamamoto explained, Japan provides "a growing reservoir of potential financial assistance," for Japanese businessmen have become increasingly interested in "the question of sharing global responsibilities." Through collaborative projects with foreign donors, "Japanese foundations will be further encouraged to come into the international arena."

In order to bolster his case, Yamamoto pointed to specific examples of international collaborative ventures, such as the jointly funded Ford and Japan Securities Scholarship Foundation project of fellowship support for the American Council of Learned Societies. A series of social science fellowships was launched by Ford and the Toyota Foundation and later joined by the Japan Foundation and other funding sources. "Even within Japanese foundations there are several joint-funding projects," including the preservation of palm-leaf manuscripts in northern Thailand. Through its program of exchanges, study missions, and seminars, the Japan Center for International Exchange is "making an effort to form a new community of foundation people within Japan. It is hoped that this community will extend to other countries as well, giving rise to more joint activities in the future. This would have a very important impact as Japan tries to relate itself to the international community in a more substantial manner. Foundation representatives have a special role to play in these activities, particularly as catalysts in generating more international cooperative spirit and promoting international cooperation."

In Europe, the Hague Club is also working to foster cooperation among European foundations. One of its members, Raymond Georis of the European Cultural Foundation, suggested that the conferees "should develop a system of information sharing between different governmental, intergovernmental, and private agencies." Such a system, he explained, would benefit not only the humanities but other programmatic areas as well.

Enrique Fernandez of SOLIDARIOS in the Dominican

Republic added his perspective on the Latin American scene. "If we look at the universe of possible organizations with which to cooperate for funding cultural endeavors," he noted, "we find family and company foundations, private foundations, and associations that are formed by groups of concerned citizens who volunteer their time and financial resources to carry out the work. However, family and company foundations are not likely to devote their attention to activities in the arts and humanities, and church and private foundations are more inclined to pursue social, economic, educational, and welfare programs. Priority is currently given to urgent, basic human needs, such as the health and welfare programs for low-income people."

Fernandez pointed out that "there have not been any major efforts in the humanities, but international foundations interested in funding cultural programs would receive a very welcome reaction from foundations in Latin America and the Caribbean. . . . Some degree of exchange should take place before such a program is established," he cautioned, but he added that "a positive contribution can be achieved if those foundations that have experience in administering cultural programs would transfer that knowledge to institutions in the Third World." He strongly recommended that local university faculties be consulted before any such programs are initiated, with the clear caveat that nonuniversity programs might be more successful than massive academic undertakings. "There are a number of cultural organizations where prospective funders and collaborators would be likely to find people within the communities who are sensitive to the humanities and familiar with the capacities of local scholars." Such carefully constructed cross-national collaborative ventures—as well as new technologies and market mechanisms—may help to maximize the resources available for cultural endeavors in an era marked by dwindling governmental outlays.

FOUNDATIONS AND CULTURAL DEVELOPMENT IN THE THIRD WORLD

The conference's liveliest discussions accompanied Francis X. Sutton's presentation on cultural development in the Third World. The need for such programs in developing nations, the dangers inherent in such work, and the question whether it is possible, or even desirable, to formulate a common cultural policy for foundation programs in the Third World all generated vigorous debate. The session opened with some preliminary comments from Sutton which highlighted the major points of his paper.

Sutton was careful to point out that "the approaches that have been characteristic of foundations, government, and everybody else who has been concerned with these things have come from various motivations. The Ford Foundation, for example, has done more for the humanities in total because of its interest in international studies than it has done because of its direct concern with humanistic study as an end unto itself." This interest in turn "was motivated by a concern that the United States in the postwar era was assuming large international responsibilities, or ought to, and therefore should have a good knowledge of the places we would be concerned with. And while the great emphasis was on the social sciences and contemporary society, which got the lion's share of attention, you could not go into that sort of thing without history or literature and art. This led to an extraordinary efflorescence in American universities' attention to Third World countries."

Interest in development took many forms, and tended to focus upon education. "As I pointed out," Sutton explained, "there has been a certain kind of nervous restraint in direct attention to cultural and social development because of the effort to be neutral and technical in the spirit of international development assistance. But inevitably there are very important effects in the educational systems which were clearly central in the development of national cultures, and one could hardly be neutral toward these things."

Tourism, as well as postwar development activities, has done a great deal to focus U.S. attention on Third World cultures. This factor, of course, brings "all sorts of potential for corruption and stereotyping" in its wake—"airport art and stereotyped folk dances, with the peculiar ossification of traditions that you get in such presentations. But still tourism is a great stimulus to interest in other cultural traditions, and it is one reason why there is a legitimate interest by outsiders in what happens to a country's monuments and cultural treasures. Many of these are now regarded as possessions of the world, and there is a legitimate international as well as a national interest in them."

Political considerations played a part as well. For example:

There are questions of national prestige. People are anxious to show that they have distinguished cultural traditions. Foundations have done a lot in that area. Some of the work Ford did in the fifties was designed to show the world that the United States is not only strong and economically progressive but also cultured. So there are all kinds of motivations which come into play here, some of them of a purely humanistic interest. The need for cultural development is not just something that the poor and backward nations have to worry about. It is a constant concern for all of us, as individuals and as citizens of countries. I would like to make the point that we are not likely to do enough if we confine our interest purely to the advancement of humanistic scholarship or cultural activities for their own sakes. We must not scorn the instrumental use of the humanities, and we are likely to do more for them if we accept that we must often justify support of them through their service of our other program purposes.

Sutton then went on to make a special plea for cultural preservation, "because that is a very neglected area and a matter of great concern to all parts of the world." An increasing amount of attention has been devoted to this type of activity in recent years in the United States, where "having come through the great period of modernism, we are all now seeking the historic and an increased sense of our heritage." However, "it is in the Third World that the needs seem to be the most abundant and very badly neglected. And doing things that are easily within the resources of even moderate-sized foundations can make a big difference. Contemporary cultural development is not simply preserving physical monuments. If you preserve the dance, it can only be done in a way that somehow keeps it alive in contemporary performance and as such has an impact on contemporary cultural development."

In response to Sutton's commentary, Enrique Fernandez painted the dangers, as well as the attractions, of cultural development in the Third World. "It is very much a national enterprise whenever you move into another culture," he noted, "and you have to realize that you are walking into someone else's territory." Although "cultural development by First World foundations is the way to achieve a certain degree of understanding of one culture by another, there is a tremendous potential for disruption as well." One clear risk is cultural contamination, in which "very rich cultures" can be "almost totally destroyed. . . . The very instruments that the specialists handle, the tape recorder or camera or video equipment, tend to bring about perceptions that are totally new to the culture under investigation."

Moreover, scholarly interest often generates waves of tourism in its wake, opening the floodgates to "people who have no respect for the culture or lack the sensitivity and training to understand it—an influx of disrespectful curiosity seekers. The professional who is doing the research may be very respectful of the people he is investigating, but the people who go after him may have a negative impact, because the scholar has contributed to the popularization of the culture that he is investigating." Academic arrogance, too, presents its perils. "Having a Ph.D. from a great American or European university, one tends to think that he or she knows everything, and should be able to understand everything. But there are true cultural differences that might eventually make it impossible to comprehend the area totally. You have to have a degree of respect that will allow you to stop short of writing about something because you realize that you are unable to comprehend it yet. And that takes quite a bit of courage, as well as a good measure of appreciation for what you are trying to study."

Fernandez also attacked the tendency to study foreign areas in order to promote nationalistic or imperialistic goals. "The more aware people become of these types of situations, the more walls they are going to build against their cultures from within," he warned. In contrast to the massive undertakings which marked many of the earlier efforts of U.S. foundations, to succeed now "you have to be on a very small, people-to-people basis in order to avoid manipulation." Latin American universities, which served as the focus for a variety of postwar programs, may have been "the wrong place because universities tend to be, in many of these countries, elitist organizations, factories of professional people who are seeking better jobs." Ironically, many of these countries now have "thousands of unemployed people with professional degrees, many more than in the United States." In fact, Fernandez extended his argument a step further with the contention that "the majority of universities in Latin America and other Third World countries are not the natural places for the humanities to be fostered. Universities provide technical and professional services. The humanities generally have not been nurtured or fostered by these institutions. What activity there has been has developed out of personal interest or by non–academically affiliated institutions." Moreover, "one has to respect national sovereignty. Cultural development is relevant precisely because it attempts to harmonize indigenous values with modernization. As such, it is very important, because it can help to smooth the transitions inherent in the development process."

Yet, to be successful, Fernandez continued, development must be an organic process. "You have to let institutions mature and people become prepared, to have a reasonable result. It is not a matter of pouring in money by the ton. That is not how to achieve cultural development." Successful programs can be "important to the stability of nations" and "can help to facilitate modernization efforts that governments want to bring about in their own countries, in order to achieve harmonious growth and adequate progress. It is important to ensure that modernization does not disrupt the indigenous cultural processes and developments that have been taking place in some countries for centuries." The case for this form of cultural endeavor must be made as quickly and cogently as possible "to the world, and to the governments which are cutting down on the humanities. This is the justification for the argument that humanistic endeavors are worth funding, and unless we present the case with renewed urgency little funding is likely to be forthcoming." Reiterating a theme presented in earlier discussions, Fernandez announced that "humanists lack that potential for selling their work to the rest of the world. They do not impress the relevance of their work on other people. There is a need for more clarity and force and urgency in these fields; the needs have to be made clearer and in a more forceful way."

Fernandez also cited the need to develop a "global culture to promote understanding between nations." Following Sutton's lead, he dissected possible foundation motives and suggested some appropriate roles that they might play. In addition to the desire to improve the general quality of life, he suggested the presence of other, more selfish aims which may often undergird such activities, including the desire to widen and exploit new market areas. To be successful, cultural development must be based on "a respectful relationship between foundations and the governments," rather than exploitation. Optimally, First World foundations should "lead the way and show other organizations how they can contribute to cultural development in their own countries. You who have been financing humanistic endeavors in your own nations can let foundations and funding agencies in the Third World know how it is to be done." Other possible roles include filling gaps left by local governments and "providing assistance for activities that are not being financed by local institutions." Partnership is an important element in these activities, as is a scrupulous willingness to avoid the "pitfalls of colonialism."

Finally, Fernandez advised foundations to work through small programs, "where you can start to learn—almost a people-to-people type of contact—but nothing big or major."

Belen Abreu enthusiastically concurred, emphasizing the potentially constructive role such efforts might play. In the Philippines, she noted, "we are always criticized for having a Coca-Cola culture. But underneath, the culture of the country is there waiting to be studied and strengthened." Foundations, of course, should not "just come into the country; we must ask them to come. . . . The developing countries should be frank enough, candid enough, and humble enough, even though their civilizations may be older, to admit that they need assistance, and they should not feel a sense of inferiority just because they are asking for help." Once there, donors should limit themselves to small grants, which she deemed "better because they involve more direct, person-to-person contact. This is more idealistic than funding the citadels of the universities."

Kazue Iwamoto of the Toyota Foundation agreed and vividly outlined the potential roles and benefits of modest programs. "Small grants can achieve unexpectedly good results if the program is well conceived and effectively managed. Large foundations can support projects conducted by governments or regional bodies and international organizations. They can provide fellowships and help universities establish new departments. Small foundations can leave such programs to their larger counterparts and governments. Small foundations should focus on other kinds of programs. They can make significant contributions to projects conducted in local universities, which can change the flow of information from developing countries to developed nations, and they can help to initiate projects to enhance the national identities of the people. Seed money can also be provided for projects of great potential."

"Our foundation in Israel has many examples of small grants

which have had great impact," added Gideon Paz of the America-Israel Cultural Foundation. "I am very much in favor of not looking down on small, and sometimes very small, grants. The people who request these grants do not have any other place to turn to, and so a foundation like this can fill a very important role." This attitude is particularly appropriate for nations like Israel, where small foundations are the norm. As Paz pointed out, although the annual allocations of his organization run to only about $1,250,000, "it is still the largest nongovernmental source of funds for the arts in Israel." Although the large foundations have traditionally played the most visible role in privately funded ventures in developing nations, Iwamoto's and Paz's comments highlighted the fact that small foundations are also well suited for such work.

Abreu applauded the notion of cultural preservation, but was less sanguine about the value of traditional humanistic studies. "In my part of the world," she confessed, "it is very hard going to find where we are when it comes to the humanities. We are still at a stage where we are worrying about whether to write in our own language or English or Spanish." To date, the humanities have taken a very low priority in the government's educational policies, since "what is important is the day-to-day business of living." Even so, "there is a serious feeling that there is a need for the humanities." For example, debates are currently afoot about whether the young should listen to American music "or Filipino, to Asian music or to the classics, which are not ours." Although central to many issues of national identity, the role of humanistic endeavor is complicated by the unsuitability of transposed Western institutions. For example, "the First Lady has dotted Manila with all kinds of museums, for the arts, for costumes, and so on. But you hardly see people go in. Somehow, there is no enthusiasm for them." Publication programs also reach only limited audiences. As Abreu explained, "We are not a reading people; we are a talking people." Promoters of the humanities, she argued, must find inventive ways of making their programs more relevant to the everyday lives of people in the communities.

Others defended the creation and maintenance of traditional cultural concerns. As Kazue Iwamoto pointed out, "I have recently been traveling in Southeast Asian countries, and during the course of my travels I have noticed the importance of encouraging the humanities because they are closely related to the identity of the people there."

Meriel Wilmot pressed the case for scholarly and literary exchanges, particularly in Southeast Asia. "The Chinese are book-hungry," she asserted. "You cannot send too many books to China, since as a result of the cultural revolution there has been a dearth of material available to them on Europe and America. They are hungry for all written matter."

Wilmot also mentioned the benefits of student exchange, a point with which Francis X. Sutton enthusiastically agreed. "It's quite obvious that no satisfactory cultural development can occur without that sort of exchange," he conceded, adding that "American foundations have been very much involved in Chinese exchanges."

Gideon Paz emphasized the need to train indigenous scholars and curators, for "one has to give them the tools, one has to train researchers, one has to train explorers from within the different cultures to do the research themselves. I think that's the only way that they will gain their self-pride." African nations, for example, "want the rest of the world to respect their culture, to know about their culture, and to see that culture explored." In light of these trends, "one of the main purposes of foundation work should be either bringing teachers to the countries or bringing students from Third World countries to the United States and other Western countries to teach them how to do their own research, how to do the preservation themselves. I think that this would be the most important work that can be done by foreign foundations, because it would mitigate the fear that the First World is trying to exercise power and influence over the less-developed nations."

W. McNeil Lowry agreed about the importance of scholarly exchanges, but added a significant qualification. When a scholar is chosen for study in another country, he asserted, the selection "must be accompanied by the condition that he or she sees it as a natural career stage, and that the person has some idea of the next stage in the pursuit of this study, research, or development as a scholar." Lowry was speaking from experience, for during his long tenure at the Ford Foundation, he directed "a program where study abroad was only undertaken when it fitted into the career profile that the artist or scholar wanted."

Shifting the focus of the discussion somewhat, Sutton noted that "we have not addressed ourselves to the rather large questions of the content and character of what I would call broadly liberal education in the Third World. And the situation is not very good. In my paper I alluded to the extent to which university education is excessively professional. For the kind of personal development that ought to be a humanistic education, most Third World universities are very poor indeed, and not much is being done about that. There are good reasons—it is difficult to do."

At this point, Tadashi Yamamoto introduced a note of skepticism, warning that "we have to be very clear in providing rationales for such assistance. There is a crying need in these developing countries for agricultural development, medical improvements—all of which require massive amounts of outside funding. I think we have to make it quite clear how such programs would fit into the development strategies of these countries."

Belen Abreu quickly seized upon this point, maintaining that "the humanities do not have a place of importance in the development process. No one could be more interested than we in the preservation of our own culture. And yet we have to worry about basic needs which take a higher priority." In many instances, the benefits of traditional humanistic study were not immediately apparent, for "when we talk of disciplines other than archaeology, we almost inevitably move out of the world of the general public and everyday community life into the world of scholarship and learning which is centered on the universities. How can we marry development needs and the needs of ordinary people with the needs of scholars? How can we get funding for humanistic programs without at the same time neglecting the needs of the communities?" What is needed, Abreu concluded, are programs which will make traditional scholarship "more direct and visible for community needs."

Taking a cue from Abreu's discourse, Gideon Paz provided additional examples from the Middle East. He declared that the King Tut show was sent abroad "in order to satisfy a legitimate and laudable curiosity of Western peoples to see these enormous treasures of ancient Egypt. What good did this do for Egypt, except to stimulate a very general interest in the country and its history? For the millions of people in Egypt, it didn't do a thing. They have not seen these treasures. The museum in Cairo is very neglected, and very few of the forty or fifty million Egyptians go to visit it." Instead, he noted, "it would have been much better to spend those millions of dollars in trying to bring knowledge about their heritage to the Egyptians themselves. Had the government done so, it would have been much more useful for the people of Egypt."

Like Paz, Abreu urged foundations to supply the "missing link" which would enable humanists to relate more directly "what they have gathered in the universities to the public at large." By way of example, she recounted the activities of a Filipino musicologist who "went from one village to another, into the gymnasiums and town plazas, giving very simple lectures on the various types of classical music." In the process, his activities served as a kind of "bridge where somebody who has been trained in the humanities has crossed the barrier and brought his discipline more directly and more visibly to the people in the communities." Through projects such as this, "the prospective donor can see that he is reaching two bases at once."

At this point, Joel Colton intervened to take up the cudgels for the traditional humanist:

> Just as we don't like to see foundations push Third World countries and Third World cultures in one direction or another, so I think we have to be careful also about the way we push humanists. There are scholars in the humanities, thinkers and writers, who have to be allowed to pursue the subjects in which they have acquired great skill, and have a contribution to make. In the long run, society will be a different kind of society if these people have an atmosphere in which they can work and the resources with which they can pursue their research. Some foundations have encouraged these scholars to use their research and their wisdom to try to help us understand some of the dilemmas of our world and give us some kind of perspective, some kind of philosophical, cultural, or historical insight into the problems that we face. Their work does have a message for contemporary society, and I would hope ideally that foundations and other sources, including educational agencies, would help both types of humanists.

Undaunted, Abreu replied that "humanists should not stay in their ivory towers. They should go down and wet their feet in the realities of everyday life. Being endowed with the advantages of a good education, they should be able to translate their findings into meaningful terms which would touch the lives of the people. So I hope that the foundations will not work just to enhance these disciplines, but to see how they can translate humanistic research to the broader public."

In his concluding remarks, Francis X. Sutton conceded that

Tadashi Yamamoto and Belen Abreu have brought up something that bothers all of us in this business. Why should we be worried about the humanities when people are hungry? But we are not in our time going to lift everybody to the GNP level of Sweden or Germany. Nations are not going to be entirely cured of the problems of poverty. They are not all going to get rich. Indeed, that is the fate of much of the world. So most people are going to have to live their lives within quite limited economic circumstances. Yet these lives must be made worthwhile in their own time. Thus there seems to me a false dichotomy in suggesting that we must make a radical choice between attending to the basic economic needs of people and their cultural needs (unless we are reduced simply to fighting famine or disaster). Development seems to me intrinsically to involve making people's lives worthwhile within what is available to them, as well as raising their incomes. This certainly means that we don't all have to run out into the villages, and turn our backs on the humanities in the universities. It should be remembered that there are opportunities to operate directly with people at quite local and traditional levels while using the scholarship and techniques of the modern humanities.

CONCLUSION

The discussions ended as they had begun, divided between those who would nurture humanistic talent within the universities and those who wish to bring the benefits of cultural study to society at large. A constant theme was the need for better communication both of the scholar's mission and of scholarly findings. Skepticism was continually voiced about the need to fund cultural endeavors in developing nations, and optimism was posited about the humanist's potential contributions in the modern world. That the effects of governmental retrenchment are being felt in every corner of the globe was clear, as was the fact that these withdrawals have caused foundations to reassess their positions and roles within the total funding picture. The dilemma of the "pioneers and pensioners" will undoubtedly be an issue of increasing concern in the coming decade. In light of these trends, new types of funding may have to be developed to sustain the programs which foundations initiate but are unable to transfer to public sponsorship. Shared technologies, market mechanisms, international collaboration, imaginative efforts to stimulate institutional self-support, and the refinement of more modest ventures are some of the techniques which may be tested in the humanities, as in other fields.

Although little consensus was reached about the need for or efficacy of a common foundation program for cultural development in the Third World, the lure and possible contributions of such work were clearly limned, particularly in the area of cultural preservation. The case for university development was less clear, with a sharply defined fissure emerging between Western representatives, who argued for the value of such programs, and participants from less-developed nations, who pleaded the case for modest programs, modest goals, and more effective community outreach activities. Yet, despite the continuing lack of consensus on the appropriate focus for foundation activities, most of the participants agreed with Francis X. Sutton's claim that the attempt to enrich people's lives culturally within their own lifetimes is a legitimate and necessary foundation pursuit.

Conclusions

Charitable trusts were born in the Old World and matured in the New. Predicated on research, expertise, flexibility, a commitment to pioneering, and fundamental social change, modern foundations have appeared in increasing numbers throughout the world since the Second World War, particularly in Europe and Japan, with scattered interest in areas as far-flung as Latin America, Australia, and the Philippines. For most, cultural endeavors have been only a minority interest, international collaboration is still in the initial stages, and budgets remain small. Yet despite variations in local philanthropic traditions, legal infrastructures, and funding patterns, many of these organizations have come to share the same concerns.

Speculation about the changing role of foundations vis-à-vis governments threaded through many of the conference presentations and discussions. In the United States, major federal cutbacks were being debated in the capitol and in the press as the conference was taking place; in other nations, such as the United Kingdom, the cuts had already occurred. Against this backdrop, foundation representatives from the United States, Europe, Latin America, Asia, and Australia shared their concern that the combined effects of governmental retrenchment and economic duress would cast foundations in a more curatorial role, providing ongoing support for the most necessary institutions in lieu of initiating fundamental social change. Ronald C. Tress of the Leverhulme Trust labeled it the dilemma of the "pioneers and pensioners"; Waldemar Nielsen sketched a broad range of possible alternatives; Otto Häfner outlined several responses already implemented by Germany's Volkswagen Foundation; and Australia's Meriel Wilmot questioned the ethics of initiating programs which government clearly will not sustain.

Areas such as the humanities seem particularly vulnerable in times of political change and economic duress. In the United States, as elsewhere, cultural and scholarly activities have been a minority foundation interest at best, overshadowed by more technically oriented educational, social welfare, scientific, and development aims. There have, of course, been exceptions, including a variety of imaginative grant-making efforts described in this book. Yet on the whole the humanities have benefited only marginally from the postwar upsurge in foundation largesse. Moreover, support from many of the leading foundations has diminished in recent years. Rockefeller Foundation outlays for the humanities peaked in constant dollars by the mid-1960s, as did those of Ford. Despite the growing importance of business giving, few U.S. corporations fund the humanities, which are often perceived as being irrelevant to business concerns. Government, rather than private largesse, has been the primary patron of scholarly and cultural endeavors in many parts of the world. Those humanities programs which have received foundation funding have also drawn their share of criticism, particularly in less-developed countries, where charges of intellectual imperialism, cultural contamination, and misguided educational initiatives have helped to tarnish the humanist's role in the development process.

Why, then, support the humanities? The answers were many and varied. Humanistic inquiry can open dialogues with other cultures, promoting mutual understanding through a clearer sense of foreign values, ideas, and aspirations. Linguistic training can reinforce national cohesion in younger, more heterogeneous nations, it can facilitate technology transfer, raise literacy rates, and aid multinational corporate marketing strategies. By facilitating the scholarly pursuit of excellence, it is possible to keep alive the spark of individual expression and freedom of inquiry, even in totalitarian regimes. Humanistic study can give an added dimension to the social sciences and the drive to understand, and ultimately redress, social ills. Clearer comprehension of foreign values, histories, and traditions can enable nations to function more effectively within the international arena, while understanding these issues at home can reinforce and delineate a nation's identity. At the individual level, a better comprehension of one's own society and the world beyond can immeasurably enrich the lives which medical and agricultural reforms have helped to safeguard and extend.

What should foundations do to further these trends? Perhaps the most common recommendation concerned the need for better communication. Although several international foundation conferences have been held in recent years, and many useful compendia published, the need for greater communication between U.S. and foreign donors working in the same fields is marked. To date, current information on worldwide foundation funding activities, particularly in specific areas such as the humanities, has been only intermittently available and fragmentary at best. One of the most promising innovations in this area is the recent reorganization of the Committee for International Grantmakers under the sponsorship of the Council on Foundations, with the expressed goal of strengthening the lines of communication among foreign and U.S. grant makers and donors interested in international fields.

The participants continually underscored the need to have humanists present their case more lucidly and persistently to donors, policy makers, and the public at large. As they explained, the benefits offered by humanistic inquiry in the furtherance of national, foundation, or corporate aims cannot simply be assumed. The rationale for corporate support should be more thoughtfully articulated, and foundations should assume a stronger advocacy role in discussions of public and private support for the humanities. At a different level, more creative efforts are needed to share the fruits of humanistic inquiry with the general public through translation programs, better media programming, and locally based outreach activities.

Several suggestions for corporate initiatives were mapped out, ranging from support of area and linguistic studies which might complement multinational marketing strategies to the application of in-kind donations (such as donated computer time) to reduce the costs of scholarly communication. The need to clarify the "fit" between corporate self-interest and the humanities was reiterated again and again.

Cultural development was another area of common interest. The notion that First World foundations should adopt a common mandate for cultural philanthropy in less-developed nations was roundly, indeed almost unanimously, rejected. While some participants questioned the appropriateness of such ventures in areas in which basic human needs were still being met, others argued that intellectual development is among the most basic of needs and thus merits a share of funding. Programs were suggested on a variety of levels, ranging from large-scale restorations of national treasures to fellowships and curatorial and archival training which would enable indigenous scholars to preserve and interpret their national heritage themselves. Participants from less-developed areas criticized the massive university-based programs of the 1960s and 1970s, arguing instead for modestly scaled village-based projects developed in conjunction with local scholars and policy makers.

As Kazue Iwamoto pointed out, both large and small foundations have a potentially beneficial role to play in such programs. Small foundations can develop and test well-defined pilot projects which might then be amplified by larger donors such as Rockefeller, Volkswagen, or Ford, much as these foundations have traditionally tested programs which were then turned over to government financing. In the process, small grant makers (that is, the bulk of the foundation community both in the United States and abroad) can complement, rather than compete with or be subsumed by, the activities of their larger counterparts.

Several specific domestic activities were also recommended. More, certainly, needs to be done to save the best of the "lost" generation of scholars, whether through the creation of independent research facilities, through fellowship programs, or through projects designed to inculcate more marketable skills. Some fields in area studies, including Africa and the Middle East, have been badly neglected, and although foundation-initiated translation programs have been extremely successful in popularizing the work of Latin American writers, possibilities for such activities in other areas of the world abound. Nor do such programs have to be the work of private foundations. The Mobil Corporation's Pegasus Award is a prime example of how a corporation can blend enlightened self-interest with humanistic concerns. Whether dealing with the realm of scholarly inquiry, village-based outreach, or cultural preservation, however, the participants concurred that the emphasis should be on excellence, rather than political concerns.

Three decades ago, Abraham Flexner complained that foundations had neglected the humanities. Then, as now, cultural inquiry played only a marginal role in foundation activities. The foundation community has grown more populous since Flexner's time, and more heterogeneous as well, to the point at which it is now international in scope. In Europe, Latin America, Asia, Australia, and the United States, grant makers are currently grappling with the implications of economic recession and governmental retrenchment, the need for better information, and the search for more equitable cross-cultural collaborative arrangements. Yet while interest in agricultural, educational, and scientific experimentation is widespread, funding for humanistic pursuits has been limited at best. In an era of shrinking public and private resources, special efforts must be made to help the humanities become more competitive for funding, to publicize their case better, to document the extent to which they are presently underfunded, and to devise more ingenious means of maximizing the impact of monetary and nonmonetary donations, both large and small, in their service. Through efforts such as these, cultural philanthropy may begin to assume a more meaningful priority on the international funding agenda.

Biographical Sketches of Contributors

OTTO HÄFNER heads the Department of Humanities and Social Sciences at the Volkswagen Foundation in Hannover, Federal Republic of Germany.

KAZUE IWAMOTO is a program officer with the Toyota Foundation in Tokyo, where she directs international grant-making activities and the "Know Our Neighbors" Translation-Publication Program.

W. McNEIL LOWRY headed the Arts and Humanities Division of the Ford Foundation for nearly two decades. The author and editor of numerous studies of the arts, humanities, and American philanthropy, he now directs his own consulting firm in New York City.

KATHLEEN D. McCARTHY served as a Visiting Research Fellow in the Humanities Division of the Rockefeller Foundation and as a consultant with the National Endowment for the Humanities; she is currently a program associate at the Metropolitan Life Foundation. She is the author of *Noblesse Oblige: Charity and Cultural Philanthropy in Chicago, 1849–1929* (Chicago: University of Chicago Press, 1982), and several articles on the history of philanthropy and the contemporary funding scene.

MALCOLM RICHARDSON, a consultant with the National Endowment for the Humanities, was named the first Visiting Research Fellow in the Humanities Division of the Rockefeller Foundation in 1977. Since then he has worked with various human rights organizations and recently completed a study of the Rockefeller Foundation's humanities program.

DANELLA SCHIFFER is the Corporate Liaison Officer of the Carnegie Corporation, a new position created by the corporation to identify issues of mutual concern to Carnegie and the corporate community and to develop working relationships and collaborative funding initiatives. Prior to her appointment at Carnegie, she worked as an industrial psychologist at Citibank, where she directed the Urban Affairs/Human Resources Division and the Loaned Executives and Professionals Program.

FRANCIS X. SUTTON is a former Deputy Vice-President of the Ford Foundation. After joining the staff of the Ford Foundation in 1954, he served in a variety of capacities, including Program Associate for the Middle East–Africa Program, field representative to East and Central Africa, and Officer-in-Charge of the European and International Affairs Program. He is the author of *The American Business Creed* (Cambridge: Harvard University Press, 1956) and of many articles on development, philanthropy, and educational concerns.

RONALD C. TRESS is the director of Britain's Leverhulme Trust. An economist, he was previously head of one of the constituent colleges of the University of London, and he has served on a range of committees on educational and African colonial affairs.

Participants

Miss Belen Abreu
Ramon Magasaysay Award Foundation
Manila, Philippines

Dr. Henry Cavanna
Fondation Internationale des Sciences Humaines
Paris, France

Dr. Joel Colton
The Rockefeller Foundation
New York, N.Y., USA

Mr. Enrique Fernandez
SOLIDARIOS
Santo Domingo, Dominican Republic

Dr. R. Georis
Fondation Européenne de la Culture
Amsterdam, Holland

Mr. Giovanni Granaglia
Fondazione Giovanni Agnelli
Turin, Italy

Mr. Otto Häfner
Stiftung Volkswagenwerk
Hannover, Federal Republic of Germany

Mr. Wolgang Heisenberg
Stiftung Fritz Thyssen
Cologne, Federal Republic of Germany

Miss Kazue Iwamoto
Toyota Foundation
Tokyo, Japan

Mr. Ian Lancaster
Calouste Gulbenkian Foundation, U.K. and Commonwealth Branch
London, England

Dr. W. McNeil Lowry
Consultant
New York, N.Y., USA

Dr. Kathleen D. McCarthy
The Rockefeller Foundation
New York, N.Y., USA

Mr. Waldemar A. Nielsen
The Aspen Institute
New York, N.Y., USA

Mr. Gideon Paz
America-Israel Cultural Foundation
Tel-Aviv, Israel

Dr. Malcolm Richardson
The Rockefeller Foundation
New York, N.Y., USA

Dr. Danella Schiffer
Carnegie Corporation of New York
New York, N.Y., USA

Dr. Francis X. Sutton
The Ford Foundation
New York, N.Y., USA

Dr. Nils-Eric Svensson
Riksbankens Jubileumsfond
Stockholm, Sweden

Dr. R. C. Tress
Leverhulme Trust Fund
London, England

Professor Erh. J. C. Waespi
Stiftung für Europäische Sprach- und-Bildungs-Zentren
Zurich, Switzerland

Miss Meriel Wilmot
Myer Foundation
Melbourne, Vic., Australia

Mr. Tadashi Yamamoto
Japan Center for International Exchange
Tokyo, Japan

Bibliographical Essay

No single source exists for those wishing to study either recent international philanthropic developments or the relationship of these trends to cultural activities. However, a range of primary and secondary sources is available which outlines the contours of selected national and foreign endeavors. U.S. and foreign annual reports are among the most useful sources of raw data on foundation programs and priorities. The Ford, Rockefeller, Andrew W. Mellon, Exxon Education, Luce, and Tinker foundations and the Carnegie Corporation, the Lilly Endowment, the Rockefeller Brothers Fund, and the JDR 3rd Fund regularly publish such reports. The Bank of Sweden Tercentenary Foundation; the European Cultural Foundation; the Leverhulme Trust; and the Gulbenkian, Myer, Toyota, and Volkswagen foundations are among the international donors to the humanities which publish reports in English. The regularly issued newsletters of the European Cultural Foundation and the Toyota Foundation's Occasional Reports are also distributed in the United States.

Several directories describe foundation activities in various parts of the world, and some occasionally include brief discussions of national policies governing foundation activities and factors affecting foundation growth. Two of the best examples of this genre are the *Guide to European Foundations* (Turin: Fondazione Giovanni Agnelli, 1978) and H. V. Hodson, ed., *The International Foundation Directory* (London: Europa Publications, 1979). Other, more specialized compendiums include *Foundation Profiles* (The Hague Club, 1981); *The Association of Australian Philanthropic Trusts* (n.p., 1981); E. K. Hart and C. A. Brown, *Directory of Philanthropic Trusts in Australia* (Hawthorne, Vic.: Australian Council for Educational Research, 1974); SOLIDARIOS, *Catalogo de Institutiones de Desarrollo sin Fines de Lucro en American Latina* (Santo Domingo: SOLIDARIOS, 1981); *Fundaciónes Privades de Venezuela* (Caracas: Fundación Eugenio Mendoza, 1973); and Narzalina Z. Lim, *Philippine Directory of Foundations* (Manila: Association of Foundations, 1974). For an overview of the U.S. scene, Waldemar A. Nielsen's *The Big Foundations* (New York: Columbia University Press, 1972) and the regularly updated *Foundation Center Source Book Profiles* (New York: The Foundation Center) are indispensable.

Studies of developments in specific parts of the world are limited in number and uneven in quality, and they often contain badly outdated information—all problems which underscore the need for more sustained and systematic inquiry into international philanthropic trends. Two U.S. commentaries which are of interest in this context are Jonathan Kendall's prematurely pessimistic article "Private Charity Going Out of Style in West Europe's Welfare States," *New York Times,* July 2, 1978, p.

1, col. 1, and the National Endowment for the Humanities report *Foreign Nations' Support for the Humanities* (Washington, D.C.: National Endowment for the Humanities, 1979). The latter document is particularly interesting, for it clearly illustrates the need for more uniform data on public and private support for the humanities.

Specific information on European developments is fragmentary, at best. In addition to the Hodson and Agnelli guides previously cited, several studies that address the issues with varying degrees of sophistication can be cited: Gothard I. Gambke's commentary entitled "The Special Role and Problems of a Foundation Established by the State," *Universitas* 16, no. 4 (1974): 303–19; Carlo Rognoni, "Europe Discovers Foundations," *Atlas World Press Review* 21 (July 1974): 33–34; Michel Pomey, *Traité des fondations d'utilité publique* (Paris: Presses Universitaires de France, 1980); *The Support of the Sciences and Humanities in West Germany and the United States* (Bloomington, Ind.: Institute for German Studies, 1977); Werner Seifart, "The Support of Research by German Foundations: Functional and Legal Aspects," *Minerva* 19, no. 1 (Spring 1981): 72–91; European Science Foundation, *The Organisation of Research in the Humanities in Western Europe* (Strasbourg: European Science Foundation, 1979); Mary Mauksch, *Corporate Voluntary Contributions in Europe* (New York: The Conference Board, 1982); Ynso Scholten, *The European Cultural Foundation: Silver Jubilee, 1954–1979* (Brussels: European Cooperative Fund, 1979); British American Arts Association, *Tax Policy and Private Support for the Arts in the United States, Canada and Great Britain* (London: British American Arts Association, 1981); and Engin Ural, *Foundations in Turkey* (Ankara: Development Fund of Turkey, 1978). David Owen's *English Philanthropy, 1660–1960* (Cambridge: Harvard University Press, 1964), one of the few scholarly studies, is particularly thoughtful and well executed, sketching the entire spectrum of British largesse over the last three centuries.

Japanese foundation philanthropy is of more recent vintage. As a result, the available works on this subject tend to be more current, conveying the exciting sense of a phenomenon still in the process of evolution. Accounts range from the macro to the micro levels. Minoru Tanaka's *Foundations in Japan: Their Legal Provisions and Tax Regulations* (Tokyo: Japan Center for International Exchange [JCIE], 1975) was one of the earliest studies commissioned by the JCIE, providing the data base on which many later undertakings were built. Subsequent developments have been thoughtfully detailed by the center's director, Tadashi Yamamoto, in *Philanthropy in Japan: A Summary Report on the Survey on Japanese Foundations* (Tokyo: JCIE, 1978), pp. 3–18, and by the U.S. representative of the JCIE, Peter Kamura, in his speech "Philanthropy in Japan and Japan's International Role," delivered at the thirty-third annual conference on the Council on Foundation in Detroit, 1982.

Kazue Iwamoto's essay "Message from the International Divison Program Officer: The Know Our Neighbors Translation-Publication Program—Its Progress and Status," in *The Toyota Foundation Occasional Report No. 1,* August 1981, provides a detailed analysis of the development of a single, highly successful Japanese foundation program of humanistic support, while Thomas R. Havens's study, *Artist and Patron in Postwar Japan* (Princeton, N.J.: Princeton University Press, 1982) affords an overview of public and private activities within a single field.

In contrast to the growing literature on Japanese philanthropy, the sources on Latin American trends are abysmally limited. The best, and indeed the only, source in English is the now-outdated Russell Sage Foundation study *Philanthropic Foundations in Latin America* (New York: Russell Sage Foundation, 1968), edited by Ann Stromberg. *Foundation News* has also regularly published articles on international philanthropic developments over the years, including a few essays on Latin America, such as Nathaniel Spear III, "Venezuela's Philanthropic Climate," vol. 13, no. 6 (November–December 1972): 31–34; and Patricia Bowers, "Fundaciónes: Foundations in Venezuela," vol. 9, no. 3 (May 1968): 73–76. For other countries covered in *Foundation News,* see Nathaniel Spear III, "Corporate Philanthropy in Japan," vol. 11, no. 5 (September–October 1970): 180–82, "Foundations of Singapore and Malaysia," vol. 12, no. 4 (July 1971): 152–53, and "The Tata Trusts: A Microcosm of India," vol. 12, no. 6 (November–December 1971): 250–52; Robert Grant and Clifton G. Metzner, "European Foundations and Research," vol. 7, no. 3 (May 1966): 45–46; and Joseph C. Kiger, "Foundations and International Affairs," vol. 6, no. 4 (July 1965): 65–68. Particularly incisive and informative contributions to *Foundation News* are Tadashi Yamamoto's "Philanthropy in Japan: Memorandum from Tokyo," vol. 16, no. 1 (February 1975): 36–39; and Datus C. Smith's "Foundations in Asia," vol. 10, no. 4 (July–August 1969): 133–39, and "Japanese Private Philanthropy," vol. 21, no. 3 (May–June 1980): 29–32.

U.S. foundations have published copiously on their activities, although few of these sources deal directly with the humanities. Many studies were penned by foundation personnel and provide firsthand accounts by the participants themselves. In this category are Melvin J. Fox, *Language Education in Developing Countries: The Changing Role of the Ford Foundation* (Remarks adapted from statement prepared for ALSED Roundtable, UNESCO, May 1974; New York: Ford Foundation, n.d.); Robert A. Mayer, *Archives in Developing Countries: The Role of Philanthropic Foundations* (Paper delivered at the annual meeting of the Society of American Archivists, 1971; New York: Ford Foundation, n.d.); and Stephen Stackpole, *Carnegie Corporation: Commonwealth Program: Travel Grants, 1947–1962* (New York: Carnegie Corporation, 1963).

Francis X. Sutton's numerous writings are particularly insightful. See, for example, his *American Foundations and Public Management in Developing Countries* (New York: Ford Foundation, 1977); "Cultural Implications of Aid Programs" (Paper delivered at the Truman International Conference on Technical Assistance and Development, Hebrew University, Jerusalem, May 1970); "Internationalizing Higher Education: A United States Approach" (Paper delivered at the conference "The International Role of the University in the 1970s," University of Massachusetts, Amherst, 1973); *Funding for International Education* (New York: Ford Foundation, 1975); *The Role of Foundations in Development* (College Station: Texas A&M University, 1982); and "The Ford Foundation and African Studies," coauthored with David Smock, *Issue: A Quarterly Journal of Opinion* (Summer–Fall 1976), reprinted by the Ford Foundation in 1976.

The Ford Foundation has issued from New York a series of pamphlets on its activities in various parts of the world, including *Ford Foundation Assistance in the Arab Middle East and North Africa* (1979); *Ford Foundation Assistance in Eastern and Southern Africa* (n.d.); and *Ford Foundation: Indonesia* (n.d.). The JDR 3rd Fund also published a useful account of its activities in *The JDR 3rd Fund in Asia, 1963–1975* (New York, 1977). Two timely overviews of recent international funding activities are Sheila Arvin McLean, *An Assessment for Grantmaking International* (New York: Grantmaking International, 1982); and Landrum R. Bolling and Craig Smith, *Private Foreign Aid: U.S. Philanthropy for Relief and Development* (Boulder, Colo.: Westview Press, 1982).

There are also a range of more general accounts, many of which were written by foundation presidents, program directors, founders, and advisers. Included among this genre are *The Foundation Watcher*, by former Foundation Center president F. Emerson Andrews (Lancaster, Pa.: Franklin and Marshall College, 1973); Abraham Flexner, *Funds and Foundations: Their Policies, Past and Present* (New York: Harper and Bros., 1952); Frederic Taylor Gates, *Chapters in My Life* (New York: Free Press, 1977); John D. Rockefeller, *Random Reminiscences of Men and Events* (Garden City, N.Y.: Doubleday, Doran and Co., 1937); Edwin R. Embree and Julia Waxman, *Investment in People: The Story of the Julius Rosenwald Fund* (New York: Harper and Row, 1949); Raymond B. Fosdick, *The Story of the Rockefeller Foundation, 1913–1950* (New York, Harper and Bros., 1952); George W. Gray, *Education on an International Scale: A History of the International Education Board* (New York: Harcourt, Brace and Co., 1941); Kenneth W. Thompson, *Foreign Assistance: A View from the Private Sector* (Notre Dame, Ind.: University of Notre Dame Press, 1972); E. Jefferson Murphy, *Creative Philanthropy: Carnegie Corporation and Africa, 1953–1973* (New York: Teachers College Press, Columbia University, 1976); Warren Weaver, *U.S. Philanthropic Foundations: Their History, Structure, Management, and Record*

(New York: Harper and Row, 1967); and Dwight McDonald's difficult-to-obtain history *The Ford Foundation: The Men and the Millions* (New York: Reynal and Co., 1956).

Other accounts of specific programs include John Ettling, *The Germ of Laziness: Rockefeller Philanthropy and Public Health in the New South* (Cambridge: Harvard University Press, 1981); Mary Brown Bulloch, *An American Transplant: The Rockefeller Foundation and the Peking Union Medical College* (Berkeley: University of California Press, 1980); Laurence D. Stifel, Ralph R. Davidson, and James S. Coleman, "Agencies of Diffusion: A Case Study of the Rockefeller Foundation," in *Social Sciences and Public Policy in the Developing World,* ed. Laurence D. Stifel et al. (Toronto: D. C. Heath and Co., 1982), pp. 57–82; Robert E. Kohler, "The Management of Science: The Experience of Warren Weaver and the RF Program in Molecular Biology," *Minerva* 14, no. 3 (Autumn 1976): 279–306; and Kohler's "A Policy for the Advancement of Science: The Rockefeller Foundation, 1924–1929," *Minerva* 16, no. 4 (Winter 1978): 480–515.

The contributions of able historians like Robert Kohler reveal the limited but growing interest among professionally trained scholars in the history of American philanthropy, both at the individual level and among foundations. Two of the pioneers in this field were Robert H. Bremner and Merle Curti. Anyone interested in the field should study Bremner's *American Philanthropy* (Chicago: University of Chicago Press, 1960) and *The Public Good: Philanthropy and Welfare in the Civil War Era* (New York: Alfred A. Knopf, 1980); and Curti's *American Philanthropy Abroad: A History* (New Brunswick, N.J.: Rutgers University Press, 1963) and *Philanthropy in the Shaping of American Higher Education,* coauthored with Roderick Nash (New Brunswick, N.J.: Rutgers University Press, 1965). Foster Rhea Dulles's *The American Red Cross* (New York: Harper and Bros., 1950) is another example of the work of the first generation of historians of philanthropy in the United States. One aspect which has consistently attracted scholarly attention is biography. Joseph Frazier Wall's outstanding portrait, *Andrew Carnegie* (New York: Oxford University Press, 1970), is a particularly compelling example of the biographer's fascination with American altruists.

More recently, historians have begun to examine the implications of private giving for health, social welfare, and charitable and moral reform agencies, and to assay the impact of the welfare state and foundation giving on research and public policy. See, for example, Scott M. Cutlip, *Fund-Raising in the United States: Its Role in America's Philanthropy* (New Brunswick, N.J.: Rutgers University Press, 1965); George M. Fredrickson, *The Inner Civil War: Northern Intellectuals and the Crisis of the Union* (New York: Harper and Row, 1965); Barry D. Karl, "Philanthropy, Policy Planning and the Bureaucratization of the Democratic Ideal," *Daedalus* 105, no. 4 (Fall 1976): 129–49; Kathleen D.

McCarthy, *Noblesse Oblige: Charity and Cultural Philanthropy in Chicago, 1849–1929* (Chicago: University of Chicago Press, 1982); Barry D. Karl and Stanley N. Katz, "The American Private Philanthropic Foundation and the Public Sphere, 1890–1930," *Minerva* 19, no. 2 (Summer 1981): 236–70, Walter S. Trattner, *From Poor Law to Welfare State: A History of Social Welfare in America* (New York: Free Press, 1974); and Howard S. Miller, *Dollars for Research: Science and Its Patrons in Nineteenth Century America* (Seattle: University of Washington Press, 1970). Contemporary commentaries, such as Waldemar A. Nielsen's *The Endangered Sector* (New York: Columbia University Press, 1979), shed light on the implications of more recent governmental expansion.

Despite these promising signs, the study of philanthropy remains in its infancy. Great amounts of work need to be done not only for U.S. historical and contemporary trends but for the international scene as well. At present, information on non-U.S. trends is woefully inadequate and fragmented, particularly if one examines specific fields such as the humanities. Despite its importance, the study of U.S. and international philanthropy has yet to receive the attention it deserves.

Habits of the Heart